Why "Bible Study" Doesn't Work

The epic failure of evangelicalism's favorite discipleship method — and how YOUR CHURCH can do something about it.

Dr. Gerry Lewis

Acknowledgements

Books don't just pop into existence, nor are they solely the work of a solitary author. The list of those whose input has influenced this book is longer than I really even know, but some absolutely must be mentioned.

The concept of the book was born out of three conversations. In one of our weekly "buddy coaching" sessions, my friend, George Steere, mentioned in passing that he wished he had just one class that was really focused on making disciples. That statement set the wheels in motion for the content of this book and inspired the "One class" approach I mention in the Epilogue.

Another friend, Tim Tolosa, invited me to come to his church to lead a training session for Sunday School workers. My preparation of that session led to the creation of the rough outline of this book and the title "Why Bible Study Doesn't Work."

A third friend, Ford McElroy, also invited me to come train his Sunday School workers. That session was the first time I presented "10 Commandments for Powerfully Effective Sunday School groups."

All of this preparation came together when I polled my email subscriber list and my Facebook community and asked what book I should write next. I'm grateful to them for giving me the motivation to write this one.

I want to especially thank my daughter, Tova Lewis Dad, who has served as my proofreader and editor for every book I have written since she was 18 years old. Since leaving her career as a high school English teacher to be a stay-at-home mom, she has served as my virtual assistant in charge of all things related to Life Matters Publications.

This book also marks the first time that Eva Dee Lewis (my Mrs. Sweetie for 32 years and counting) has given me an additional pair of eyes on a book manuscript. I'm not sure why I waited so long because her input was insightful and invaluable.

Finally, I want to thank Chandler Bolt and the Self-Publishing School community for giving me new tools to take my writing and publishing to a completely new level. Included in the SPS experience are: my writing/publishing coach R.E. Vance, editor H. Elaine Roughton, and cover designer Happy Self Publishing (project manager Sushmitha Naroor). And I can't leave without mentioning the great mutual support, inspiration, and encouragement of the SPS Facebook community.

To Eva – Sweetie, you are the love of my life and my partner in everything that is good. Thank you for saying, "Yes" and "I Do."

To Tova, Zeke, Joe, and Allie – What amazing grownups you are! I never could have imagined how cool it would be to see my kids become parents.

To Aziza and Owen (born during the final editing of this book) – Grandpa is my favorite name!

To Jesus – Thank You for Your wonderful and amazing grace and for calling me to this journey. What a ride!

Introduction

I wonder how many people stopped reading when they saw the title of this book.

Really? This guy doesn't believe in Bible study? He must be one of those liberal and shallow self-help guys who just uses a few verses out of context to make his topic work.

No, my friends, that is not the case. I believe the Bible. I believe every bit of it. I believe every word of it. I believe the Bible is completely reliable, trustworthy, accurate, and true in ALL matters of faith, practice, and history. I believe that the Bible is God's written revelation of Himself. I love this description found in one statement of faith: the Bible is "truth without mixture of error."[1]

I believe in studying the Bible. In fact, in the first chapter of this book, entitled "Why Should We Study the Bible?" I argue that studying the Bible is essential. I believe in it and I do it. I have degrees from two seminaries (and they didn't mess me up!) that taught me how to study, teach, and apply the Bible. I spent 25 years — 20 as senior pastor — on the staff of local churches, teaching people how to study the Bible so that they might hear God and put His word into practice in their daily living. I believe that studying the Bible is crucial in the life of a follower of Jesus!

What I don't believe is "join another Bible study group and you'll be more like Jesus."

---

[1] The Baptist Faith and Message, 1963

Now, I've never heard anyone say it exactly like that, but the message from the church is often clear: the answer to everything is more prayer and Bible study. Go to more prayer meetings, pray longer on your own, get in as many Bible studies as possible ... *maybe if we keep you busy enough praying and studying the Bible you won't have time to sin!*

Let me ask you a question. If more (or better) Bible studies is really the answer, how in the world do we have so many people who:

- Have gone to Sunday School for decades
- Have attended, helped in, and taught Vacation Bible School
- Have participated in multiple 13-week or 40-day video-based Bible study courses
- **And are Biblically illiterate and don't have any idea how to *think* or *live* Biblically?**

It seems that we have a disconnect somewhere.

I'd like to offer, in this brief book, a way of rethinking Bible study. A way that refocuses studying the Bible with the intent of making disciples. A way that emphasizes not just the "what" of Bible study, but also the "how" and the "why" of studying the Bible.

There are two primary groups of people for whom I wrote this book, though I will be really happy when *anyone* reads it. I wrote this book for **pastors and church leaders** who are seeking direction and inspiration for making disciples and developing leaders. These pastors and leaders are seeking to give direction to the small groups in their churches and they truly want their group Bible studies to be impactful.

I also wrote this book for **group Bible study leaders**. Actually, this is whom I really had in mind when I decided to undertake this project. I want to inspire and empower these valuable ministry leaders in their strategic role in the disciple-making ministry of their local churches.

I'll begin, as I have already mentioned, in Chapter 1 with "Why Should We Study the Bible?" This will certainly not be an exhaustive exposition of the Scriptural admonitions for the study of God's word. Rather, I will be highlighting some basic fundamentals on why studying the Bible is essential to the life of a follower of Jesus.

In Chapter 2 — "A Blueprint for a Jesus-Focused Church" — I will be sharing my personal touchstone concepts for why the church exists: The Great Commission, The Great Commandment, and A New Commandment.

In Chapter 3 — "What's Missing in Our Bible Studies?" — I will highlight where I think the disconnect has occurred and why "Bible study" has failed as a strategy for making disciples.

In Chapter 4 — "Transforming 'Bible Study' into Disciple Making" — I will offer some ideas for rebooting our methods and strategic processes for studying the Bible that can help us move our focus from knowledge accumulation to life transformation.

Finally, in Chapter 5 — "Cleanup On the Bible Study Aisle!" — I will share two practical and simple methods of group Bible study that can infuse new life into your groups.

If I haven't lost you already, I'm taking that as a good sign. Let's take a moment and pray:

> *Lord, open our eyes to see YOU*
> *Open our ears to hear YOU*

Open our minds to know YOU
Open our hearts to love YOU
Speak, Lord, Your servants are listening.

Let the adventure begin ...

Chapter 1 - Why Should We Study the Bible?

Spiritual Vegetables

So, why should a follower of Jesus study the Bible? Because it's good for you! There, I've said it! That's all the reason you need. It's the broccoli of the Christian life. It's full of vitamins and minerals and... green stuff ...

(I really like broccoli, by the way.)

Unfortunately, I think we may have been guilty of giving that kind of answer. It's the go-to answer for every spiritual question: you need more prayer and Bible study. You need to eat more vegetables.

My son, with whom I enjoy devouring a wide variety of foods, has a particular opinion about vegetables. He says that vegetables are what food eats. He believes that mashed potatoes, mushrooms, and jalapeños (not necessarily eaten together) provide him with all the "vegetables" necessary.

Eat more vegetables! Why? Because everyone should eat more vegetables!

Study the Bible and pray more! Why? Because everyone should study the Bible and pray more!

Vegetables are not an end in themselves, but a means to an end. The end is **health** and vegetables are the best source of some forms of nourishment that lead to health.

Some may call my next statement heresy (especially in the current climate where the "h" word is batted around like a

Ping Pong ball), but I want to suggest that prayer and Bible study are not ends in themselves either.

Prayer and Bible study are a means to the end of **spiritual health** through deep and personal connection to God, resulting in living out what I have come to call the "*Christ-life*." I will talk more about that in Chapter 3.

Spiritual Health

So what does this *spiritually healthy Christ-life* look like and how does studying the Bible help us move toward it?

Let me remind you that the scope of this book does not allow for an exhaustive exploration of all the benefits of studying God's word. That is for another time, another place, and probably another author.

I've selected six representative passages that are some of the most familiar. My reasoning for picking the familiar passages is that we don't necessarily need new information; we need new perspective.

With each of these passages, I have included 3 to 4 various translations to get a sense of the diverse textures and flavors brought out by different Bible scholars.

Psalm 119:11 - Heart preparation

(NASB) - *Your word I have treasured in my heart, that I may not sin against You.*

(KJV) *Thy word have I hid in mine heart, that I might not sin against thee.*

(ESV) *I have stored up your word in my heart, that I might not sin against you.*

(Voice) *Deep within me I have hidden Your word so that I will never sin against You.*

Sin is such an ugly word. We really don't like to use it unless we are talking about someone else. And then, we would really like to limit it to "big ticket items" like murder and adultery (unless the person committing adultery is someone we really like, in which case they made an unfortunate mistake because they were only human).

But the Bible actually describes a lot of things that are sinful, and they are not all external actions. In fact, every external sinful action began with an internal sinful attitude or decision. A good way of saying that is that **sin begins in the heart**. When the Bible talks about the heart, it is not referring to the blood-pumping organ. Neither is it referring to a simply emotional response. Biblically, the heart is where decisions and choices are made.

So, how do we make sure that we are making good, spiritually healthy decisions and choices? We do that by making sure that our hearts are filled with God's revelation of Himself and His purposes.

To *treasure*, *store up*, and *hide* God's word deep within us is to have constant access. In moments of temptation, we usually don't have time to look up a Bible verse to see what God says about a particular situation. So, to have God's word tucked away within our hearts gives us that access.

In some cases, that means a passage of Scripture we have studied and memorized. That is a really good way of treasuring God's word in our hearts. In other cases, it is an intimate and deep knowledge of the character of God, even if a specific verse doesn't come to mind.

None of us is born with that deep and intimate knowledge of God's character. Neither do we simply absorb it by osmosis by being in the company of other Christ-followers. It comes through deep and intimate interaction with God through prayer and studying Him in His word.

So, one spiritual health benefit of studying the Bible is that *it affects the condition of our hearts and helps us navigate the rough waters of temptation to sin.*

Psalm 119:105 - Clarity of purpose

(NASB) - *Your word is a lamp to my feet and a light to my path.*

(NLT) - *Your word is a lamp to guide my feet and a light for my path.*

(MSG) - *By your words I can see where I'm going; they throw a beam of light on my dark path.*

Have you ever been on one of those cave tours where they get everyone close together and turn off all the lights so you can experience total darkness? It doesn't take very many seconds for it to become pretty disconcerting.

We really weren't made for darkness.

In the dark, we are likely to stumble over unseen hazards. In the dark, we are likely to make wrong turns, because we can't see the right path. In the dark, I have stubbed my toes, bruised my shins, walked into walls, tripped over suitcases, and hesitated to move forward because of fear of what might be in the dark. Darkness can be frustrating and scary.

But, what a difference a little light makes! Imagined ghouls disappear. Real hazards can now be identified and avoided. The path becomes clearer. Work and play become possible. All because someone turned on a bit of light.

Spiritual darkness can be frustrating and scary, too. We can be in a well-lit room and yet be paralyzed by the realization that we really don't know what to do next. If we are Christ-followers, we sometimes can be paralyzed with the fear that we might do the wrong thing and miss God's will.[2] We can imagine scary outcomes and missed opportunities.

This verse reminds us that we have light available to us. God's word can serve as a lamp to guide us and help us see where we are going. It shines a light on our dark path and helps us see more clearly.

That sounds good, doesn't it? If we will just study the Bible enough, we will have the answer to every question and we will know what to do in every situation.

Oops! I think I just told you to eat more vegetables again.

Your word is a lamp to my *feet* and a light to my *path*. *Path* implies direction. *Path* implies progress, movement, and journey. *Feet* implies where I am on that journey. I want to suggest that this verse is not promising us that

---

[2] I addressed this fear in my eBook, *On God's Back Porch: Resting In and Enjoying God's Will When You Don't Have Specific Directions.* (drgerrylewis.com/backporch)

studying God's word will give us the answer to every question we ever have. It is saying that studying God's word will help us see more clearly where we are and will help us make progress toward God's preferred direction for us.

*When Jesus spoke again to the people, he said, "**I am the light of the world.** Whoever follows me will never walk in darkness, but will have the light of life."*
(John 8:12, emphasis added)

In God's written self-revelation, we discover the character of God's ultimate self-revelation: Jesus.

*In the beginning was the **Word**, and the **Word** was with God, and the **Word** was God. He was with God in the beginning. Through him all things were made; without him nothing was made that has been made. In him was life, and **that life was the light of all mankind** ... The **Word** became flesh and made his dwelling among us. We have seen his glory, the glory of the **one and only Son**, who came from the Father, full of grace and truth.*
(John 1:1-4, 14, emphasis added)

The source of the light for our path is the One who is our companion on the journey. So, a second spiritual health benefit of studying God's word is that ***we gain a greater understanding of God's Word (Jesus), learning more of His character and purpose, so that we can display that character on every step of the journey.***

Hebrews 4:12 - Deep look inward

(NASB) - *For the word of God is living and active and sharper than any two-edged sword, and piercing as far as the division of soul and spirit, of both joints and marrow, and able to judge the thoughts and intentions of the heart.*

(NLT) - *For the word of God is alive and powerful. It is sharper than the sharpest two-edged sword, cutting between soul and spirit, between joint and marrow. It exposes our innermost thoughts and desires.*

(AMP) - *For the word of God is living and active and full of power [making it operative, energizing, and effective]. It is sharper than any two-edged sword, penetrating as far as the division of the soul and spirit [the completeness of a person], and of both joints and marrow [the deepest parts of our nature], exposing and judging the very thoughts and intentions of the heart.*

My son, the carnivore (or the anti-vegetarian) has been a collector of knives and swords for most of his life. Before he was old enough to have sharp ones, he had plastic and wooden ones. He's always been all boy.

I once had a conversation with a friend whose kids were about the same age as mine. He was concerned about his son's fascination (he called it an obsession) with knives and guns. He was worried that there might be something wrong and that this obsession with weapons was an indicator that he might have a propensity toward violence.

I don't really know about his son, but mine is one of the most gentle and kind men I know. His fascination is with *weapons*, not *violence*, and he has a clear appreciation and understanding of their different usages.

I think we may not have a full understanding of this whole two-edged sword concept when it comes to the word of God. The imagery of the passage isn't referring to a weapon of warfare, but an instrument used by the high priest in the Old Testament sacrificial system. The word translated as "sword" was used of a short sword or dagger used in sacrifice or the knife (scalpel) used by a surgeon.

The context of the passage helps us to understand that we are talking about the priest's role and tools in the act of sacrifice. Notice the next two verses:

And there is no creature hidden from His sight, but all things are open and laid bare to the eyes of Him with whom we have to do. Therefore, since we have a great high priest who has passed through the heavens, Jesus the Son of God, let us hold fast our confession.
(Hebrews 4:13-14)

The word of God is not an ancient, dusty, out-of-date book that has nothing to do with 21st Century living. God's word is the vibrant (living) expression of God's self-revelation. God's word is powerfully at work (active) because God's Word (Jesus) is alive and at work eternally. The sharpness of the sword in the hands of our great high priest is enough to lay us bare to the very core — down to the marrow, where life flows.

Frank Viola says it this way in his book, *Jesus Now: Unveiling the present day ministry of Christ:*

Jesus Christ, by His living word and through His indwelling life, enables us to differentiate between our soul (our mind, will, and emotion) and our spirit (the deepest part of us where God dwells). To put it another way, part of the high priestly ministry of Christ is to reveal what comes from our own thoughts, feelings, and volition and what comes from His leading...

Specifically, the writer likens each of us to be a sacrifice on the altar. Under the Old Testament covenant, when

17

Israel offered up sacrifices, the sacrifice was tied to an altar. The priest killed it with a very sharp knife, dividing the sacrifice into two halves. The word translated "sword" in Hebrews 4:12 is machaira, *and one of the meanings is "a large knife, used for killing animals and cutting up flesh." The priest's knife was so sharp that it pierced the sacrifice to the joints and the marrow. As a result, all the insides of the sacrifice that were once hidden could now be seen. They were laid bare without concealment. After the priest opened the sacrifice with his knife, he would burn it with fire as an offering to the Lord ...*

As the sacrifice was opened with the knife of the Old Testament priest so that the joints and marrow were all laid bare, the Lord Jesus does this same penetrating, exposing, and dividing work on our spirits and souls with the knife of His word. It's no accident that Revelation 1:16 says of Christ, "Out of his mouth went a sharp two-edged sword." In like manner, Revelation 2:12 says, "To the angel of the church in Pergamum write: These are the words of him [Jesus] who has the sharp, double-edged sword." As our Great High Priest, the Lord Jesus uses His word to pierce and divide every part of us: the spiritual from the soulish. Only the sharp sword of God's word handled by the Lord Jesus Christ can clearly discern the source of our living. Just as a human knife can divide bone from marrow, the knife of God's word can divide the closely-knit spirit from the soul.

Within an immature Christian or one who operates in his or her flesh, it's virtually impossible to distinguish between what comes from a person's own natural soul (mind, will, or emotion) and what comes from their spirit (the place where God dwells, speaks, and reveals). In other words, such a person can't tell when God is speaking to them and when it's their own fallen thoughts, emotions, or desires that they assume is God's speaking. The word of

God, when received with a teachable ear and an unhardened heart (see Hebrews 3), proves sharper than any two-edged sword. Hebrews 4:12 says the word of God is "living." It's not dead or inanimate, but something that is vital and speaks yesterday, today, and forever.[3]

That is a lengthy quote and requires some good spiritual teeth to chew on it, but I think the point is well made (better by Frank than by me) that a third spiritual health benefit of studying God's word is that **we avail ourselves to the work of Jesus, making us aware of who we really are at the depths of our being.**

2 Timothy 3:16-17 - Equipped for purpose

(NASB) - *All Scripture is inspired by God and profitable for teaching, for reproof, for correction, for training in righteousness; so that the man of God may be adequate, equipped for every good work.*

(ESV) - *All Scripture is breathed out by God and profitable for teaching, for reproof, for correction, and for training in righteousness, that the man of God may be complete, equipped for every good work.*

(NLT) - *All Scripture is inspired by God and is useful to teach us what is true and to make us realize what is wrong in our lives. It corrects us when we are wrong and teaches us to do what is right. God uses it to prepare and equip his people to do every good work.*

When I was a pastor, I once preached a series of Sunday evening sermons entitled, "What Good Is the Bible?" where

---

[3] I first heard this on Frank Viola's podcast. More can be found at frankviola.org/2014/04/29/hebrews412.

I highlighted a passage of Scripture from each book of the Bible and illustrated a practical life lesson. It wasn't a spectacular sermon series — as much as that pains me to admit — but I did succeed in making the point that every book of the Bible really does have something practical to say about how we live our lives in every era.

One reason the Bible speaks to our lives is because of its Source. The Bible is "inspired" or "breathed out" by God. There are varying interpretations of what the *inspiration* of Scripture entails. It is not my intent here to conduct a thorough study of the nature of inspiration, but it might help to mention a couple of approaches. Some believe that inspiration means that God virtually dictated the words of Scripture to those who wrote it down. Others believe that God inspired the writers to write, but they used their own words.

I think we can even make a case for variety within the means of inspiration. The point is that God was deeply involved in the process of the recording, preserving, and collecting the ancient texts that now make up what we know as our Bible.

It is also worth noting that, since what we know as the *New Testament* was in the process of being written, that the Apostle Paul was referencing the *Old Testament* (the Hebrew Scriptures and their Greek translation, the Septuagint) in this letter to Timothy. He would have had no clue that his own words here would one day be considered a part of "All Scripture."

That doesn't mean that we should not consider the New Testament writings as Scripture. On the contrary! But it *does* mean that in the New Testament writings, we get to be flies on the wall and observe God's unfolding of His self-revelation in its fullest expression.

20

Now, with that bit of explanation, let's get to the heart of this passage. I want you to notice that the Bible is profitable (useful) for teaching us what we should and should not do (adjusting our behavior to God's standards) and showing us how we should live (developing our character).

But for what purpose? What's the bottom line? Here it is: that God's people may be **equipped for every good work**.

Equipped is relatively easy to get our minds around; it has to do with preparation in advance. It is having the proper resources. But for *every* good work? How in the world can we possibly be ready and equipped for *every* good work? How do we even know what those good works are? Is there a list somewhere? Do we have to memorize every command in the Bible and do everything just like they did in the ancient world?

Back in 2007, a journalist named A.J. Jacobs released a best selling book entitled *The Year of Living Biblically*.[4] A self-described "reverent agnostic" from a Jewish background, Jacobs skillfully (and humorously) chronicled his year of trying to obey literally every command in the Bible. Though I don't share his viewpoint on the Bible, I really enjoyed the read.

I think A.J. and I would agree on one point: *a performance-based focus on keeping commands is exhausting and often frustrating*. We might compare it to calculating the precise blend of vegetables

[4] A.J. Jacobs, *The Year of Living Biblically: One Man's Humble Quest to Follow the Bible as Literally as Possible*, Simon & Schuster (2007).

necessary for the "perfect" daily diet. Now, that will get you excited about your lunch!

Could it be that the point Paul was making in his letter to his young protégé, Timothy, was that a consistently healthy diet of God's word would result in the kind of spiritual preparation that brings clarity to *each situation*? In other words, learning to adjust our behavior through deep interaction with God's written revelation will **enable us to be prepared to respond with the right spiritually healthy good work that is needed in each situation**.

2 Timothy 2:15 - Approved for visible mission

(KJV) - *Study to shew thyself approved unto God, a workman that needeth not to be ashamed, rightly dividing the word of truth.*

(NASB) - *Be diligent to present yourself approved to God as a workman who does not need to be ashamed, accurately handling the word of truth.*

(Voice) - *Timothy, do everything you can to present yourself to God as a man who is fully genuine, a worker unashamed of your mission, a guide capable of leading others along the correct path defined by the word of truth.*

If there was ever a verse that affirmed Bible "study," this one is it, right? How much clearer could it be? **Study** to show yourself approved! You want to be approved by God, unashamed as a Godly worker, rightly dividing the word of truth? **Study** is what you need!

Eat more vegetables!

The King James Version of the Bible uses the word "study" to translate the Greek word *spoudason*. Now, you will never hear me speak negatively of the KJV. I grew up with that translation, as did a lot of people. I do get a little impatient with those who insist that it is the *only* translation to use. But I also get a little impatient with those who say the same of the ESV or whatever other translation is their favorite.

This is not about what Bible translation is the best; this is about a particular translation of a particular word in a particular verse. Kind of makes me sound particular, doesn't it?

I'm not sure what the early 17th century English translators of the KJV had in mind when they translated *spoudason* as "*study*," because a clearer understanding of the meaning of *spoudason* is "*to be zealous, to be eager, to make every effort.*"

In other words, Paul's instruction here to Timothy is not directed toward a simply cognitive or intellectual exercise. It's not so much a matter of learning more through gaining more information. It is a matter of preparation through diligent and intentional focus on what matters most.

That's why I love the way The Voice Bible renders this verse: *Timothy, do everything you can [*__be diligent or zealous__] to present yourself to God as a man who is fully genuine [*__approved or tested__], a worker unashamed of your mission [*__intentionally focused__], a guide capable of leading others along the correct path defined by the word of truth [*__visibly competent in the word of God to equip others in living the Christ-life__]. [*__My commentary inserted__]*

So another spiritual health benefit of studying God's word is that *we have the opportunity to intentionally focus on our visible mission of equipping followers of Jesus.*

1 Corinthians 8:1 - Built up in love.

(NASB) - *Now concerning things sacrificed to idols, we know that we all have knowledge. Knowledge makes arrogant, but love edifies.*

(ESV) - *This "knowledge" puffs up, but love builds up.*

(NIV) - *But knowledge puffs up while love builds up.*

(NLT) - *But while knowledge makes us feel important, it is love that strengthens the church.*

I can't leave the subject of spiritual health without addressing the key motivator that protects us from getting too proud of our Biblical knowledge. That motivator is **love**.

Some people really love vegetables. In fact, they love them so much that they decide the only way to be really healthy is to stop eating meat and to eat only vegetables. They become vegetarians and they tout the benefits of vegetarianism. They spend time researching all the health benefits of vegetarianism. They find books and articles about vegetarianism and they share them in hopes that they can convince more people to be vegetarians. That's all great!

But there's a more important issue than the health benefits of vegetarianism. Does the vegetarian become so proud of his superior diet that he treats meat eaters with contempt?

Does she place more emphasis on vegetarianism than she does on people?

Is it possible that we can become so proud of all the Biblical knowledge we have gained through our "Bible studies" that we forget to meet people with the love and grace of Jesus? *If our Bible knowledge doesn't result in Christ-like behavior, should we really be proud of that knowledge?*

Is it really healthy?

RECAP - So, why should we study the Bible?

In this chapter, we've reinforced 5 spiritual health benefits of studying God's word.

1. It affects the condition of our hearts and helps us navigate the rough waters of temptation to sin. (Psalm 119:11)
2. We gain a greater understanding of God's Word, learning more of His character and purpose, so that we can display that character on every step of the journey. (Psalm 119:105)
3. We avail ourselves to the work of Jesus in showing us ourselves at the depths of who we really are. (Hebrews 4:12)
4. It enables us to be prepared to respond with the right spiritually healthy good work that is needed in each situation. (2 Timothy 3:16-17)
5. We have the opportunity to intentionally focus on our visible mission of equipping followers of Jesus. (2 Timothy 2:15)

And all this is to be *carried out in love*. That's really important as we move into the next chapter and consider what this looks like corporately in a group known as the church.

Chapter 2 - A Blueprint for a Jesus-Focused Church

On June 1, 2008, I began a new chapter in my life and ministry. That was my first day as Executive Director/Director of Missions of Harvest Baptist Association, a regional network of churches in north central Texas. I moved my books, file cabinets, diplomas, a few pieces of furniture, and 20+ years of ministry memorabilia out of the pastor's office/study at Eagle Mountain Baptist Church, where I had been senior pastor for 17 years.

My new office was a little smaller than my previous one, so I had to do some downsizing. To be honest, my new office was an unattractive and unwelcoming room in an old, unattractive, and ill-equipped building. I spent the first few weeks repainting and re-staging almost the entire building, both inside and out. We really needed a better facility, but we were making the most of what we had as we planned for the future.

The future came sooner than we anticipated. On July 10, 2010, I stood in the middle of the street at 3:00 a.m. and watched that building (and all my belongings) burn to the ground. And so, the 22-month building program began. That's enough of that story. I can feel my stress level rising just writing these few lines about it.

If you are going to construct a building, you need a good set of plans designed by someone who knows construction. If you are building a church *building*, you need a set of plans drawn by an architect or draftsman who can bring your vision to reality.

If you are building a *church*, you need a set of plans given by the *Head* of the church, so that *His* vision can be brought to reality.

The Foundation

Now when Jesus came into the district of Caesarea Philippi, He was asking His disciples, "Who do people say that the Son of Man is?" And they said, "Some say John the Baptist; and others, Elijah; but still others, Jeremiah, or one of the prophets." He said to them, "But who do you say that I am?" Simon Peter answered, "You are the Christ, the Son of the living God." And Jesus said to him, "Blessed are you, Simon Barjona, because flesh and blood did not reveal this to you, but My Father who is in heaven. I also say to you that you are Peter, and upon this rock I will build My church; and the gates of Hades will not overpower it.

(Matthew 16:13-18)

Upon this rock *I* will build *My* church ...

That little phrase highlights two things we can never — ever — forget regarding the church. The first one is that *Jesus is building the church*. We may be working, planning, strategizing, praying, enlisting, giving... you get the point... but it is Jesus who is building. Our part is to join Him and cooperate with Him in the work that He is doing.

He doesn't need our help, but He wants our cooperation.

The second thing we can never forget is that *it is His church*. When I speak of *my* church, that's not necessarily a bad thing, as long as I am referencing the church into which I am investing my life, gifts, and passions. But if *my* church ever communicates a sense where I feel a sense of ownership or control, then, Houston, we have a problem!

In His book, *Church Unique,*[5] Will Mancini talks about "upper room" thinking. He says that every church has a "lower room" by default. This is the place of *provision.* In the lower room, we talk about *place* (the physical facilities), *personality* (leaders), *program* (ministry structures and plans), and *people* (relationships). All of these are really important and are worthy of our time and attention.

However, the room that every church does not have by default is the "upper room." This is the place of *vision.* This is the place where prayer is not a *bookend* activity (*"Sam, please open us in prayer... Lucy, please close us in prayer"*), but it is *the* activity. Our purpose is to seek *Jesus's vision* for *His* church by seeking *Him* above all else.

Check out these words from Psalm 63:

*You, God, are my God, earnestly **I seek you; I thirst for you, my whole being***
longs for you, *in a dry and parched land where there is no water.*
I have seen you *in the sanctuary and beheld your power and your glory.*
*Because your love is better than life, **my lips will glorify you**.*
*I **will praise you** as long as I live, and in your name I will lift up my hands.*

---

5 Will Mancini, *Church Unique: How Missional Leaders Cast Vision, Capture Culture, and Create Movement,* 2008, Jossey-Bass.

I will be fully satisfied, as with the richest of foods; with
*singing lips **my mouth will praise you.***

*On my bed **I remember you; I think of you** through*
the watches of the night.
Because you are my help, I sing in the shadow of your
wings.
***I cling to you;** your right hand upholds me.*

Those who want to kill me will be destroyed; they will go
down to the depths of the earth.
They will be given over to the sword and become food for
jackals.
*But the king will **rejoice in God;** all who swear by God*
will glory in him,
while the mouths of liars will be silenced.
(Psalm 63, NIV, emphasis added)

Did you notice what was missing in that Psalm? There is
no seeking of God's *will*, God's *guidance*, God's *answers*,
God's *provision*, or God's *stuff*. Certainly those can be
found elsewhere in Scripture, but in Psalm 63, the psalmist
is only seeking (and praising) *God*. As I have shared the
"upper room" concept with several different congregations,
I have become convinced that the attitude and focus
demonstrated in this psalm is the key to accessing the
upper room.

And here's the irony of it: if *we* try to build the upper
room, it automatically becomes a part of the lower room.

I will build *My* church ...

Before we move on to the plans for the *structure* of the
building, we better make sure that we are clear about the
foundation on which Jesus is building His church.

Upon **this rock**, I will build my church ...

What rock, Jesus? Are you talking about Simon *Barjona* [*son of John*], whom You had just renamed Peter [*Petros: the Rock*]? Not at all.

Jesus was talking about Peter's great confession: *"You are the Christ, the Son of the living God."*

The church's one foundation is Jesus Christ, her Lord,[6] says the old hymn. *On Christ, the solid Rock, I stand; all other ground is sinking sand,*[7] says another.

Every contractor worth his salt knows that the *foundation* is the most important part of a building. Scrimp, neglect, or cut corners on the foundation, and it really doesn't matter how great you build on top of it.

The reality of Jesus Christ — His identity, purpose, completed work on the cross, and current activity in the world — is the only foundation for a genuine, Biblical, Jesus-focused church.

If our "Bible studies" are not built upon that same foundation, they will not produce true disciples.

The Framing

Let's say we have our foundation in place. Now it is time to start building the structure on top of the foundation. We need good plans to know where to put our wall studs,

---

6 Samuel L. Stone, *"The Church's One Foundation,"* 1866.
7 Edward Mote, *"My Hope is Built* (The Solid Rock)," 1834.

ceiling joists, rafters, wiring, plumbing, duct work — all things that will be virtually unseen when the building is completed, yet they are what holds everything in place and makes the whole building function at its maximum potential.

So, what are these structures for the church? We put Jesus in His place as the foundation, so we're done with Him, right? Of course not! His *identity* is our foundation. His *words* are our framework.

So, what words of Jesus provide our framework? All of them? Well, all of them are, of course, equally valid and authoritative, but trying to figure out how to structure a church on all the words of Jesus would be a little like trying to literally obey every command in the Bible (remember A.J. Jacobs?).

This is my opinion, so I take complete responsibility for anything that lacks clarity or seems not to go deep enough, but I think there are three sayings of Jesus that can serve as the "load bearing walls" of the church. Everything else can be connected to these.

The first is what is known as **The Great Commission**.

And Jesus came up and spoke to them, saying, "All authority has been given to Me in heaven and on earth. Go therefore and make disciples of all the nations, baptizing them in the name of the Father and the Son and the Holy Spirit, teaching them to observe all that I commanded you; and lo, I am with you always, even to the end of the age."
(Matthew 28:18-20)

One of the things I do with churches is to help them with strategies to clarify their mission and vision. These concepts are crucial to help churches identify their unique role in the larger community of faith. "Copy and paste" mission or vision statements are ineffective at best.

However, there is one thing I will never do with a church: I will never help them define their unique purpose for existing. There is a reason for that. *I believe every church has the same purpose for existing, and that is to glorify God and make disciples.*

Imagine this: Jesus has been crucified and resurrected. He has been appearing to various groups of people over the course of several weeks. Apparently, He has made an appointment with the eleven remaining disciples (minus Judas) to meet at a certain place in Galilee.

They gather at the agreed upon place and time and Jesus appears to them and speaks the words recorded in Matthew 28:18-20. In this passage, He *commissions* them as *apostles* [those who are *sent*] and gives them their purpose from that day forward: **make disciples**.

Without getting too grammatically technical (there are plenty of other sources that dig much deeper into this), it is important to note that there is one imperative verb in this passage. *Matheteuo* means "make disciples." There are three participles related to the verb: *going*, *baptizing*, and *teaching*. All of these are components of the imperative — *make disciples*.

Going

The apostolic commission is to go where one is sent. That implies that we don't wait for potential disciples to come to us. We go where the people are. I've heard it said that, because *go* is a participle in the original language, it should be translated, "as you are going." I am great with that translation.

What I am not great with are some who have then concluded that there is no imperative to go. The reasoning goes this way: Since *make disciples* in the imperative and *going* is simply a participle, Jesus assumed that they would be going. Therefore, He said, in essence, "Since you are going anyway, as you are going, make disciples."

Twelve hours of New Testament Greek in Seminary does not make me a scholar, but I do know that there is such thing as an *imperatival participle*. Almost 55 years of living and almost 40 years of church ministry don't make me an expert either, but I do know that **nothing can be assumed**.

I am confident that this phrase could accurately be rendered, "*Go — and as you are going — make disciples of every people group.*" (The phrase translated *of all the nations* [*panta ta ethne*] is not to be understood geographically or nationally, but ethnically. In other words, groups of people who have a common culture and language).

Baptizing

The evangelical faith tradition that is a part of my heritage practices *believer's baptism*. That means that baptism does not provide forgiveness of sins nor does it initiate a person into the kingdom of God or the church. Baptism is for those who have been forgiven of their sins and brought into the kingdom of God through faith in Jesus Christ. It is, therefore, a visible and public identification with the community of Christ-followers.

I realize that not every branch of the evangelical tree views baptism the same way, but we pretty much all agree that baptism is a matter of identification. Part of the process of making disciples is identifying Christ followers and welcoming them into the community of those on the journey.

Baptism is a symbol, but it is not simply symbolic. To be put under the water symbolizes death. The old person — the person whose priority was self — has died and been buried. To come out of the water symbolizes resurrection and new life. The new person — the person whose priority is following Jesus — is now publicly identified with the community of faith.

Therefore if anyone is in Christ, he is a new creature; the old things passed away; behold, new things have come.
(2 Corinthians 5:17)

The fact that baptism is a symbol doesn't mean it is optional for the Christ-follower. It is a component of the disciple making commission. If a person says he wants to follow Christ and yet refuses this first step of identification with other Christ-followers, then we may legitimately question his motivation.

If a church does not take seriously the commission to help these new Christ-followers publicly identify with the community, then we may legitimately question their disciple-making identity.

Teaching

This is, in my opinion, the participle that gives us the greatest challenge in making disciples. How ironic is that? The powerful tool of teaching is actually a hindrance to discipleship!

35

How so? Glad you asked.

Look again at the words of Jesus — *"Go therefore and make disciples of all the nations, baptizing them in the name of the Father and the Son and the Holy Spirit, teaching them to observe all that I commanded you; and lo, I am with you always, even to the end of the age."*

The problem is that we keep trying to put a period in the middle of the clause. Here's what I mean:

Go, therefore and make disciples... baptizing... teaching them.

If the period goes there, we assume that we are making disciples if we have a class for them. That results in the vegetable-eating "Bible studies" that I've been referencing. Attend this 13-week "discipleship" class and when you finish, we will declare you discipled.

I grew up in Southern Baptist churches. When I was young, we had something called "Training Union." It happened on Sunday nights, and the idea was that we would be trained in Christianity and church life. (The generation before me had "Baptist Young People's Union.")

Somewhere along the way, the SBC decided to change the name to "Church Training." And a few years later, it became "Discipleship Training." Along with the demise of the Sunday evening worship service in many churches came the end of these Sunday evening "Discipleship Training" classes. In fact, I have often heard (from those who lament the loss of Sunday evening worship) that canceling Sunday evening services "killed our discipleship program."

Do you know what really has killed the discipleship program in most churches? Having a discipleship program!

Somehow, we thought having classes that we called "discipleship training" would result in discipleship. And the reason we thought that may just be because we thought there should be a period after the word *teaching*.

So, let's move the period. ... *teaching them to observe (or obey)*.

So, now we know what we are supposed to be teaching them: **obedience and submission**. Teach them respect for authority. Teach them the 10 Commandments. Teach them the rules. Teach them what they are supposed to *do*.

If any new immigrant comes to our country, one of the things they will need to learn is to observe (obey) the laws of the land. It will go much better for them if they know the rules under which our culture operates.

So, we may take the approach to making disciples that says it is the job of the church to help new Christ-followers understand the rules under which the kingdom operates. Teach them where the boundaries are. Help them understand the dos and don'ts of following Jesus. One more word study may help us get clarity. The word translated as "observe" or "obey" (depending on what translation you use) is the word *tereo* and it means, "to watch over, to guard, to hold in custody, to preserve."

It is not simply a matter of teaching them to obey the **rules** of the kingdom. It is about teaching them to preserve and watch over the **ways** of the kingdom.

"... Teaching *them to observe **all** that I commanded you*" (emphasis added). Eleven of these guys had spent 3 years with Jesus. How in the world would they be able to remember everything He commanded?

They wouldn't. And I don't think He expected them to. He didn't spend three years teaching them the rules of the kingdom to obey. He spent 3 years teaching them the ways of the kingdom to preserve. And He promised them His ongoing presence and direction through the Holy Spirit: "*and lo, I am with you always, even to the end of the age.*"

Jesus had told them earlier, "*But the Helper, the Holy Spirit, whom the Father will send in My name, He will teach you all things, and bring to your remembrance all that I said to you.*" (John 14:26)

Our goal in making disciples is not simply giving Christ-followers a checklist of rules to live by; it is equipping them to live as those who walk in step with Jesus, empowered by the Holy Spirit, and demonstrating His character in both attitude and action.

The second "load-bearing wall" is known as the ***Great Commandment***.

One of them, a lawyer, asked [Jesus] a question, testing Him, "Teacher, which is the great commandment in the Law?" And He said to him, " 'You shall love the Lord your God with all your heart, and with all your soul, and with all your mind.' This is the great and foremost commandment. The second is like it, 'You shall love your neighbor as yourself.' On these two commandments depend the whole Law and the Prophets." (Matthew 22:35-40)

What if you could learn one thing that would change everything else? What if you had one key that would unlock every door? What if there were one vegetable you could eat that would provide you with all the nutrition you would ever need? Sorry, I couldn't resist that last one.

What if there were a secret that, once learned, would make life's purpose and direction clear?

Chances are, you are familiar with what Jesus said in Matthew 22:37-40 when He was asked about the greatest commandment. His answer has been, justifiably, called the *Great Commandment*. In a nutshell, love God and love others. Easy, right? So, now we'll just move along to the next one.

Let's not move on quite yet.

Did you notice how the question of the greatest commandment originated? *"One of them, a lawyer, asked Him a question, testing Him..."* If you were to take the time to read the entire twenty-second chapter of Matthew, you would discover that Jesus was being bombarded with questions from different religious groups. These were not sincere questions seeking truth and deeper understanding. Rather, they were loaded questions, asked from hostile agendas, which were intended to discredit Him.

I've seen a few press conferences where a pack of journalists with their microphones and recorders shouted above one another asking questions of a political figure or athlete. It was obvious that they were not really interested in what the interviewee had to say. They were not looking for **truth**, but for a **story**. Their minds were already made up about the truth. They simply wanted a sound bite to use for their own purposes.

I think this illustration may give us the flavor of the context of this conversation. These groups — the Pharisees and Sadducees — had given their lives to rigorous study of and obedience to the Law of Moses (the first five books of the Old Testament). They were experts. All you had to do to know that they were experts was to ask them. They were proud of their knowledge and education and were sincere in their irritation with this un-pedigreed rabbi from Nazareth who was rocking their world with His outrageous claims to truly know the heart of God.[8]

The Pharisees and Sadducees had not only studied the commandments in the Law, they had been part of a heritage that developed a complex system of laws based on the Law. They knew how to keep rules and how to deal with rule breakers. And they knew that, if they could get Jesus to dishonor one commandment in favor of another, they would have a way to expose Him as an unschooled rabble-rouser.

Imagine their angst when He answered their question in a way that not only gave them no way to accuse Him, but also amazed and enlightened everyone who was listening. He did not simply quote one commandment from the abundance of rules. He quoted two commandments that elevated the conversation above the standard of *rules for living* to the highest standard of *God's heart for His people.*

"You shall love the Lord your God with all your heart, and with all your soul, and with all your mind." This is the great and foremost commandment. This quote from Deuteronomy 6:5 is a command to love God above all else.

---

[8] This is a perfect example of 1 Corinthians 8:1 from the previous chapter.

In fact, it is a command to love God with one's whole being. Wait! A command to love? Can you really control what or whom you love?

That, my friends, can be answered with a resounding YES! Now, if we define *love* as a *feeling* that makes your heart go *pitter patter* (or *thumpity thump* if you are "in love"), there may be some challenges. But if we define *love* as a *choice* to value, honor, bless, and seek the highest good (which is the sense of the word *agapao*), then that's another story.

This command to love God is to choose to value and honor Him above all else (with *all* your heart, *all* your soul, *all* your mind). It is to choose to give God His rightful place at the center of your existence, receiving your complete allegiance and ultimate affection. *"This,"* says Jesus, *"is the great and foremost commandment."*

This statement would not have been shocking to those who asked the question. They would have known Deuteronomy 6:5 well. They would have had it memorized. If they had been leaders in some of the congregations with whom I work, He might have even gotten a hearty, "Amen!"

But Jesus wasn't finished. His next statement was shocking, even though *"you shall love your neighbor as yourself"* was a direct quote from Leviticus 19:18. This is again a commandment with which they would have been familiar. They knew the context of Leviticus 19, that one should not hate one's countryman, bear grudges, or take revenge.

What they didn't expect was for Jesus to summarize the entire Old Testament (the Law and the Prophets) into a simple core principle: love God, love others and... are you ready for this... love self. They did not expect Him to essentially say, "If you get this right, you will understand and demonstrate God's heart for the world. You will see God, yourself, and others *as God sees*. You will fulfill God's kingdom purpose."

Two concepts bear a little extra emphasis. The first: "*Love your neighbor **as yourself**.*" There are Godly teachers and preachers — persons whose Biblical knowledge and scholarship far exceed any of my efforts — who have sometimes minimized the "self" part of this statement. It is almost as if we have another example of putting the period in the sentence where it doesn't go.

Love God; love others. God first, others second, self last. Put others first. But neither Jesus, nor Moses, said, "Love your neighbor more than you love yourself... love your neighbor better than you love yourself... love your neighbor ahead of yourself." They said, "Love your neighbor *as* yourself."

On another occasion, Jesus said, "*In everything, therefore, **treat people the same way you want them to treat you**, for this is the Law and the Prophets.*" (Matthew 7:12, emphasis added)

Here's the deal: "first" implies priority, order, preference, and hierarchy. Jesus was not commanding a preference or hierarchy of importance. Love is about how we choose to **treat** others; the ideal is to treat them the way we would like to be treated by them. If this desire is built on the foundation of loving God with all our heart, soul, and mind, then we will love others and ourselves as God intends.

His name was Cecil. I was his pastor, but I was also his friend. Cecil loved his coffee. He would enter the church building every Sunday morning, Sunday evening, and

Wednesday evening and head straight for the coffee pot. His commentary was always the same: "I haven't had a cup of coffee since I left the house." His house was about a half mile from the church and it took him about five minutes to make the trip!

Cecil also loved chili. He ate it *at least* once a day and sometimes more. I like chili once in a while. But I love coconut cream pie. Now if I were going to do for Cecil what I wanted him to do for me, I would give him a big slice of coconut cream pie, hoping that he would reciprocate. And if he were going to do for me what he wanted me to do for him, I could expect a pot of his homemade chili.

But the pie wouldn't be a blessing to him. In fact, since he was an insulin-dependent diabetic, it would have actually been harmful to him. So if I wanted to treat Cecil like I wanted to be treated, I would do for him what blessed him and treat him to his favorite meal of chili. And if he wanted to treat me the way he wanted to be treated, he would find me a pie.

The essence of loving others as ourselves is knowing what it feels like to be honored and valued, and intentionally looking for opportunities to do the same.

The second concept: "Love **your neighbor** as yourself." Who is He talking about? Let's first go back to Leviticus.

*You shall not hate **your fellow countryman** in your heart; you may surely reprove your neighbor, but shall not incur sin because of him. You shall not take vengeance, nor bear any grudge against **the sons of your people**, but you shall love your neighbor as yourself; I am the LORD.*
(Leviticus 19:17-18, emphasis added)

The religious leaders who kept coming to Jesus with their trick questions understood that they should love their fellow Jews, but they were pretty sure it was okay to hate everyone else. So, when Jesus said, *"Love your enemies and pray for those who persecute you,"* (Matthew 5:44) His words were not well received.

On another occasion, Jesus was asked a similar trick question — again by a lawyer — *"What shall I do to inherit eternal life?"* (Luke 10:5).

Instead of answering his question directly, Jesus asked him, *"What is written in the Law? How does it read to you?"*

The lawyer gave the answer that he thought Jesus was looking for, *"You shall love the LORD your God with all your heart, and with all your soul, and with all your strength, and with all your mind; and your neighbor as yourself."* (Do you think that this may have been consistently central to the core message of Jesus?)

Jesus then told him, *"You have answered correctly; do this and you will live."*

Don't miss this next part: *"But **wishing to justify himself,** he said to Jesus, 'And who is my neighbor?'"* (Emphasis added). In other words, this lawyer wanted to know the minimum requirements of this love. Who am I required to love? Who are the enemies and outsiders that I am justified in ignoring, if not outright hating?

And in answer to that, Jesus tells the parable of the Good Samaritan.

I won't take time or space to repeat the entire story here. Let me just move to the bottom line. Instead of defining who the neighbor is that we are required to love, Jesus asked who needs a neighbor to love them. That is radical! That is scandalous!

The Great Commandment says that we don't get to pick and choose **whom** we love. Our choice is **that** we love. We don't withhold love (honor, value, seeking the best) from **them**, simply because they are not **us**. To love your neighbor as yourself is to seek to **be** a neighbor to those who need it most.

The third "load-bearing wall" is a **New commandment.**

A new commandment I give to you, that you love one another, even as I have loved you, that you also love one another. By this all men will know that you are My disciples, if you have love for one another.
(John 13:34-35)

The fact that we don't pick and choose whom we love does not mean that we love everyone the same. In one of the most deeply intimate experiences Jesus shared with his disciples — the Last Supper — he delivered this new commandment. It went deeper than the "love your neighbor as yourself" commandment that He spoke to the crowds. This commandment recognized that there is something supernaturally unique about the love that exists within the company of Christ-followers.

This love is not simply love that was commanded in the Law and reiterated in the words of Jesus. This is commanded love **as modeled by Jesus**. This company of close friends and followers had experienced a level of intimacy with God-in-the-flesh that had never been experienced by anyone. They were — from that day forward — to demonstrate that kind of love among themselves.

But, it wasn't a secret, private love that they could hoard in their exclusive **J**-club, sharing a secret handshake and acknowledging each other with raised eyebrows and knowing glances. His intent was that their love would be so visible, so distinctively representative of His own character that *all men* (everyone) would know that they were followers of Jesus.

This love, demonstrated in chosen behavior and attitudes, would be **the distinguishing characteristic** of genuine Christ-followers. Not their theological orthodoxy. Not their rules for acceptable or prohibited behavior. It was their **Jesus-like love** demonstrated in the way they lived out their lives in *community*. It would demonstrate to those who are not *yet* one of us, that they *can* belong.

There is so much that we could explore in that Last Supper conversation that Jesus had with his disciples, but I want to simply highlight the "love one another" commandment. A little later in the evening — perhaps even as they walked together from the upper room to the garden of Gethsemane — Jesus reiterated this new commandment:

This is My commandment, that you love one another, just as I have loved you.
(John 15:12)

Over 25 years ago, I had an *AH-HA* moment related to this verse. In all the recorded sayings of Jesus, in all four Gospels, this is the only specific commandment that Jesus identified as His. This is the only place where He said, "My commandment." There are a few instances where He said, "My commandments" (John 14:15, John 14: 21, John 15:10) without specifically naming them. But one time only, He said, "This is My commandment..."

So how important is it to Jesus that His followers love one another? If it is **the distinguishing characteristic** of genuine Christ-followers, then do we really have an option about how we treat one another within the community of faith?

This **"one another"** concept would become so important to the early followers of Jesus that it became a constant reminder within the early church.

The Apostle Paul

- *Be devoted to one another in brotherly love; give preference to one another in honor.* (Romans 12:120)

- *Be of the same mind toward one another.* (Romans 12:16)
- *Owe nothing to anyone except to love one another.* (Romans 13:8)

- *Therefore let us not judge one another anymore, but rather determine this — not to put an obstacle or a stumbling block in a brother's way.* (Romans 14:13)

- *So then we pursue the things which make for peace and the building up of one another.* (Romans 14:19)

- *Now may the God who gives perseverance and encouragement grant you to be of the same mind with one another according to Christ Jesus.* (Romans 15:5)

- *Therefore, accept one another, just as Christ also accepted us to the glory of God.* (Romans 15:7)

- *And concerning you, my brethren, I myself also am convinced that you yourselves are full of goodness, filled with all knowledge and able also to admonish one another.* (Romans 15:14)

- *Greet one another with a holy kiss. All the churches of Christ greet you.* (Romans 16:16)

- *Actually, then, it is already a defeat for you, that you have lawsuits with one another. Why not rather be wronged? Why not rather be defrauded?* (1 Corinthians 6:7)

- *So then, my brethren, when you come together to eat, wait for one another.* (1 Corinthians 11:33)

- *So that there may be no division in the body, but that the members may have the same care for one another.* (1 Corinthians 12:25)
- *All the brethren greet you. Greet one another with a holy kiss.* (1 Corinthians 16:20)

- *Greet one another with a holy kiss.* (2 Corinthians 13:12)

- *For you were called to freedom, brethren; only do not turn your freedom into an opportunity for the flesh, but through love serve one another.* (Galatians 5:13)

- *But if you bite and devour one another, take care that you are not consumed by one another.* (Galatians 5:15)

- *Let us not become boastful, challenging one another, envying one another.* (Galatians 5:26)

- *Bear one another's burdens, and thereby fulfill the law of Christ.* (Galatians 6:2)

- *With all humility and gentleness, with patience, showing tolerance for one another in love.* (Ephesians 4:2)

- *Therefore, laying aside falsehood, speak truth each one of you with his neighbor, for we are members of one another.* (Ephesians 4:25)

- *Be kind to one another, tender-hearted, forgiving each other, just as God in Christ also has forgiven you.* (Ephesians 4:32)

- *Speaking to one another in psalms and hymns and spiritual songs, singing and making melody with your heart to the Lord.* (Ephesians 5:19)

- *And be subject to one another in the fear of Christ.* (Ephesians 5:21)

- *Do nothing from selfishness or empty conceit, but with humility of mind regard one another as more important than yourselves.* (Philippians 2:3)

- *Do not lie to one another, since you laid aside the old self with its evil practices.* (Colossians 3:9)

- *Bearing with one another, and forgiving each other, whoever has a complaint against anyone; just as the Lord forgave you, so also should you.* (Colossians 3:13)

- *Let the word of Christ richly dwell within you, with all wisdom teaching and admonishing one another with psalms and hymns and spiritual songs, singing with thankfulness in your hearts to God.* (Colossians 3:16)

- *And may the Lord cause you to increase and abound in love for one another, and for all people, just as we also do for you.* (1 Thessalonians 3:12)

- *Now as to the love of the brethren, you have no need for anyone to write to you, for you yourselves are taught by God to love one another.* (1 Thessalonians 4:9)

- *Therefore comfort one another with these words.* (1 Thessalonians 4:18)

- *Therefore encourage one another and build up one another, just as you also are doing.* (1 Thessalonians 5:11)

- *And that you esteem them very highly in love because of their work. Live in peace with one another.* (1 Thessalonians 5:13)

- *See that no one repays another with evil for evil, but always seek after that which is good for one another and for all people.* (1 Thessalonians 5:15)

- *We ought always to give thanks to God for you, brethren, as is only fitting, because your faith is greatly enlarged, and the love of each one of you toward one another grows ever greater.* (2 Thessalonians 1:3)

- *For we also once were foolish ourselves, disobedient, deceived, enslaved to various lusts and pleasures, spending our life in malice and envy, hateful, hating one another.* (Titus 3:3)

James (the half-brother of Jesus)

- *Do not speak against one another, brethren. He who speaks against a brother or judges his brother, speaks against the law and judges the law; but if you judge the law, you are not a doer of the law but a judge of it.* (James 4:11)

- *Do not complain, brethren, against one another, so that you yourselves may not be judged; behold, the Judge is standing right at the door.* (James 5:9)

- *Therefore, confess your sins to one another, and pray for one another so that you may be healed. The effective prayer of a righteous man can accomplish much.* (James 5:16)

The Apostle Peter

- *Since you have in obedience to the truth purified your souls for a sincere love of the brethren, fervently love one another from the heart.* (1 Peter 1:22)
- *Above all, keep fervent in your love for one another, because love covers a multitude of sins.* (1 Peter 4:8)

- *Be hospitable to one another without complaint.* (1 Peter 4:9)

- *As each one has received a special gift, employ it in serving one another as good stewards of the manifold grace of God.* (1 Peter 4:10)

- *You younger men, likewise, be subject to your elders; and all of you, clothe yourselves with humility toward one another, for God is opposed to the proud, but gives grace to the humble.* (1 Peter 5:5)

- *Greet one another with a kiss of love. Peace be to you all who are in Christ.* (1 Peter 5:14)

The Apostle John

- *But if we walk in the Light as He Himself is in the Light, we have fellowship with one another, and the blood of Jesus His Son cleanses us from all sin.* (1 John 1:7)

- *For this is the message which you have heard from the beginning, that we should love one another.* (1 John 3:11)

- *This is His commandment, that we believe in the name of His Son Jesus Christ, and love one another, just as He commanded us.* (1 John 3:23)

- *Beloved, let us love one another, for love is from God; and everyone who loves is born of God and knows God.* (1 John 4:7)

- *Beloved, if God so loved us, we also ought to love one another.* (1 John 4:11)

- *No one has seen God at any time; if we love one another, God abides in us, and His love is perfected in us.* (1 John 4:12)

- *Now I ask you, lady, not as though I were writing to you a new commandment, but the one which we have had from the beginning, that we love one another.* (2 John 1:5)

The Author of Hebrews

- *But encourage one another day after day, as long as it is still called "Today," so that none of you will be hardened by the deceitfulness of sin.* (Hebrews 3:13)

- *And let us consider how to stimulate one another to love and good deeds, not forsaking our own assembling together, as is the habit of some, but encouraging one another; and all the more as you see the day drawing near.* (Hebrews 10:24-25)

What were you thinking as you read through that list? Take a moment and consider your church or your Bible study group. How do you compare with the New Testament standard?

"But that was then," you might say. "They didn't have to deal with some of the people in my church! They didn't experience the challenges we experience in our current culture!"

I don't have the time — or inclination — to point out how absolutely untrue that is! Most of the people who will read this book don't realize how easy it is to follow Christ at this time compared to the first century. We absolutely live in a world of conflict and ungodliness. We absolutely live in a world of challenge. We absolutely live in a world where hostility toward Christianity is on the rise. And there are some places in the world where Christ-followers are experiencing persecution at near-Biblical levels.

But this book is not written for them. There are a couple of things that do not happen in those cultures. The idea of casual Christianity is foreign. They know following Jesus is costly and they expect it to be difficult. They also know the absolutely essential nature of *one another*. For many of them, following Christ has resulted in the loss of family, homes, jobs, possessions, and security.

Now, tell me again how hard it is for us?

I don't want to end this chapter with that hard question, so let me offer a bit of encouragement. I am not saying this "one another" stuff is easy. It's not. It takes intentionality and perseverance. It was not easy in the first century either. How do I know that? Because the New Testament writers spent so much time talking about it!

If it were automatic, or even easy, they wouldn't have had to keep bringing it up over and over again! But they did keep bringing it up over and over again because they had learned from Jesus that the church could not endure apart from this "load-bearing wall" of *one another*.

RECAP – The chief Architect's plans for His church

Jesus is building His church. *The foundation is the reality of Jesus Christ* — His identity, purpose, completed work on the cross, and current activity in the world. The load-bearing walls are:

1. **The Great Commission** – *equipping disciples* to live as those who walk in step with Jesus, empowered by the Holy Spirit, demonstrating His character in both attitude and action.

2. **The Great Commandment** – *loving God* by choosing to give Him His rightful place at the center of your existence, so that He receives your complete allegiance and ultimate affection. We are also to love our neighbors by seeking to *be* a neighbor to those who need it most.

3. **A New Commandment** – *loving one another with Jesus-like love* demonstrated in the way we live out our lives in *community*.

So far, we have reinforced five spiritual health benefits of Bible study and looked at Jesus's plans for how we develop a spiritually healthy community. Next, we will dig deeper into the disconnect between Jesus's plans and our reality.

Chapter 3 - What's Missing In our Bible Studies?

There's an old preacher joke (I'm not sure whether that means the joke is old or that it is a joke told by old preachers), that tells the story of a preacher who had one of those really embarrassing moments during his Sunday morning message.

It seems that he was one of those preachers who preached from a sermon manuscript that was several pages long. On this particular Sunday morning, he was preaching from the book of Genesis. He began a sentence with, "And Adam said to Eve..." Turning to the next page in his notes he realized that he had skipped a page. In a moment of panic, he spoke to himself — but loud enough for the congregation to hear — and appeared to finish the sentence with, "I believe I have a leaf missing!"[9]

I will pause here and let you boo, groan, or give whatever response seems appropriate.

Something is missing in our group Bible studies

Though I imagine we come to these groups with all our "leaves" in place, I believe there are three crucial components that are missing from many small group Bible

---

[9] *Then the eyes of both of them were opened, and they knew that they were naked; and they sewed fig leaves together and made themselves loin coverings.* (Genesis 3:7)

studies. As a result, we may be providing the proper Biblical vegetables, but we are not really producing healthy, developing disciples who are consistently living out the *Christ-life*.

Missing Intentionality

The first of these missing crucial components is *intentionality*. Here's a profound truth: if you don't have a target, you will miss it every time. ***The primary reason that our small group Bible studies are ineffective in producing disciples is that we have not designed them to produce disciples!***

I have neither done nor accessed any hard data on this, but I have had enough conversations with pastors and church leaders over the years to feel reasonably confident in my opinion on the perceived purpose of most Sunday School classes and other Bible study groups. If we were to ask these leaders to name the primary purpose of these groups, the majority would say that the purpose is to **study the Bible together**.

Eat more vegetables!

I'm also relatively certain that the average member of such groups, if asked the same question, would point to ***fellowship with other believers*** as the purpose of the groups. Eat more cake!

I realize that I am showing my personal bias here, but if the primary purpose of the church is to make disciples, then shouldn't every group — no matter how sweet and encouraging the fellowship — be driven by the common intentional target of making disciples?

Study the Bible together for what purpose? For the purpose of encouraging people to consistently develop their walk with Christ. Enjoy fellowship and sharing life with other believers for what purpose? For the purpose of encouraging one another and building each other up in the **Christ-life**.

When I was a young seminarian, and then a young pastor, we were taught that Sunday School was the ***primary outreach arm of the church***. That may have been true at one time, but it is true in very few churches now. But even if it were true, outreach that is simply focused on ***conversions*** and not ***disciple-making*** falls short of our Biblical mandate as the Body of Christ.

A few years ago, I was introduced to a book that was starting to make a splash. *Same Kind of Different as Me* [10] is a true story of events that took place in and around Ft. Worth, Texas. I was intrigued both by the story and the setting because it mentioned so many places with which I was familiar, having lived on the edge of Ft. Worth for all but two years of the previous quarter century.

Same Kind of Different as Me is a wonderful and compelling story. I really enjoyed it. In their second book, *What Difference Do It Make* [11], the authors peeled back the curtain on more of their unlikely friendship, including some opportunities that resulted from the first book.

---

[10] Ron Hall & Denver Moore with Lynn Vincent, *Same Kind of Different as Me: A Modern-Day Slave, An International Art Dealer, and the Unlikely Woman Who Bound Them Together*, 2006, Thomas Nelson Publishers.
[11] Ron Hall, Denver Moore, and Lynn Vincent, *What Difference Do It Make? Stories of Hope and Healing*, 2009, Thomas Nelson Publishers.

There was one particular story that stood out for me above all the rest:

One day, I asked Mr. Ron, "Mr. Ron, all these white folks be inviting us to their Bible studies. How come none of 'em's inviting us to their Bible doins?"

I ain't sayin it ain't all right to study the Bible. You got to study the Bible to know the rules of life. But I notice a lotta folks doing more lookin at the Bible than doing what it says. The book a' James says, don't just listen to what God has to say, do what He says. And Jesus said God is gon' separate us, the sheep from the goats, based on what we did, not on how much we read.[12]

Denver Moore never learned to read or write, but he spoke deep and simple truth. The passage he was referencing in the *book a' James* says,

But prove yourselves doers of the word, and not merely hearers who delude themselves. For if anyone is a hearer of the word and not a doer, he is like a man who looks at his natural face in a mirror; for once he has looked at himself and gone away, he has immediately forgotten what kind of person he was. But one who looks intently at the perfect law, the law of liberty, and abides by it, not having become a forgetful hearer but an effectual doer, this man will be blessed in what he does.
(James 1:22-25)

So, if our purpose is simply to study the Bible together, it can result in passive knowledge gainers who delude themselves into believing that Christianity can be passive and observational, rather than active and participatory. As

---

[12] *What Difference Do It Make?*, p. 152.

a result, *ministry* is left up to the *professionals* and *knowledge* of Scripture is substituted for *living* the **Christ-life**. Isn't there a better target than that?

Let's say, then, that the intentional target for our group Bible study is disciple making. What, exactly, is a disciple?

The word translated "disciple" in the New Testament (*mathetes*) means "pupil" or "learner." It was not a word that was uniquely used of those who followed Jesus. Every rabbi (teacher) had disciples. But certainly, Jesus meant that the disciples we are to make are those who are learning from and following Him.

That's what the word *disciple* means. But what is a working definition of a disciple of Jesus that gives us that intentional target for all our pursuits as the church? Nowhere in the New Testament can we find the phrase, "A disciple is _____." We only get examples of what disciples do. The fact that a specific definition is absent may be part of our issue.

I'd like to propose a possible definition. This is not *the* definition of a disciple. It is probably not even the *best* definition of a disciple. But, it is *my* working definition — based on deep study of the New Testament — and helps me define my intentional target.

A disciple is a person who is on-mission to live out the *Christ-life*. This is not simply someone who *has* a mission, but who is constantly and intentionally *on* that mission. The mission is the **Christ-life**.

So, what is the **Christ-life**? Is it to be as much like Jesus as possible? Partly. My definition includes four sub-points:

- Loving who He loves
- Obeying what He says
- Influencing the world for Him
- Demonstrating His character

But even those sub-points — as powerful and helpful as I believe them to be — are more of an indication of a Christ-*like* life than the **Christ-life**. Here's where I get the concept of the **Christ-life.**

I have been crucified with Christ; and it is no longer I who live, but Christ lives in me;
and the life which I now live in the flesh I live by faith in the Son of God,
who loved me and gave Himself up for me.
(Galatians 2:20)

For you have died and your life is hidden with Christ in God. When Christ, who is our life, is revealed, then you also will be revealed with Him in glory.
(Colossians 3:3-4)

Christ lives in me... I live by faith... I have died and my life is hidden with Christ in God... Christ, who is my life...

That, my friends, is the **Christ-life**! And that is the target of our disciple making. Can you see how that concept can transform the way we approach life as the church? Consider this powerful passage that describes the role of church leaders:

*And He gave some as apostles, and some as prophets, and some as evangelists, and some as pastors and teachers, for the **equipping of the saints for the work of service**, to the **building up of the body of Christ**; until we **all** attain to the unity of the faith, and of the*

*knowledge of the Son of God, to a **mature** man, to the* **measure of the stature which belongs to the fullness of Christ.** *As a result, we are no longer to be children, tossed here and there by waves and carried about by every wind of doctrine, by the trickery of men, by craftiness in deceitful scheming; but speaking the truth in love, we are to **grow up in all aspects into Him who is the head**, even Christ, from whom the whole body, being fitted and held together by what every joint supplies, **according to the proper working of each individual part**, causes the **growth of the body for the building up of itself in love.***
(Ephesians 4:11-16, emphasis added)

If our groups are going to be effective in disciple making, we must be **intentional** about disciple making!

Missing Accountability

The second of these missing crucial components is **accountability.** Here's another profound truth: if your vehicle doesn't have an energy source, you will eventually stop moving. The primary power of groups in the disciple-making process is the shared energy that we draw from one another in moving toward the goal of living out the **Christ-life.** If we disconnect and isolate ourselves from that energy source, we lose our spiritual momentum. **If our lives together are simply about enjoying the fellowship and not deliberately calling one another to maturity, we can begin to actually deplete the spiritual energy of the church.**

So, how should this accountability work? Let me remind you of what Jesus said in the passage known as the Great Commission: *"teaching them to obey all that I have commanded you."*

Since I addressed this in Chapter 2, I'll be brief here and just repeat one of my conclusions from that discussion: ***Our goal in making disciples is not simply giving Christ-followers a checklist of rules to live by; it is equipping them to live as those who walk in step with Jesus, empowered by the Holy Spirit, demonstrating His character in both attitude and action.***

If intentionality is the *target*, accountability is the *aiming* mechanism. It is the *external* energy source that re-aligns us toward our target of making disciples. All followers of Jesus have an *internal* energy Source — the indwelling Holy Spirit — that is our primary energy source. We might describe the Holy Spirit as our *firing* mechanism. You could say that we have everything we need to live the ***Christ-life*** because we have the presence of Christ through the indwelling Holy Spirit.

You could say that, but you would be wrong. Remember all those "one another" instructions? God made us for relationship. When God said, *"It is not good for the man to be alone,"* (Genesis 2:18), He wasn't just talking about the husband/wife relationship. He was stating an eternal principle that He would continue to unfold throughout Scripture: ***Humans were not made for isolation.***

We need each other. When our aim is off, we need each other to help us re-align and re-focus.

Two are better than one because they have a good return for their labor. For if either of them falls, the one will lift up his companion. But woe to the one who falls when there is not another to lift him up. Furthermore, if two lie down together they keep warm, but how can one be warm alone? And if one can overpower him who is alone, two

can resist him. A cord of three strands is not quickly torn apart.
(Ecclesiastes 4:9-12)

I love the imagery of the cord of three strands. It is a reminder of the mysterious and wonderful partnership that exists when we are united with one another in human relationships with Jesus as the third strand that turns a *twist* into a *braid* and holds it all together. Accountability is when we remind each other to stay firmly entwined in the braid.

That brings up another point. Accountability is sometimes seen as a threat because we are concerned about who is accountable to whom. Who gets to hold someone else accountable? To be candid, the church has often gotten this wrong by creating an authoritarian hierarchy. The key to Biblical accountability within the church is that it is mutually chosen — we hold *one another* accountable. Specific roles within the congregation are not about *authority*; they are about *responsibility*. Accountability is mutually chosen through mutual submission.

Submit to one another out of reverence for Christ.
(Ephesians 5:21, NIV)

Let's get down to where the rubber meets the road. How does this mutual accountability work in terms of re-aligning and re-focusing one another in living the **Christ-life**? A couple of passages come to mind for me.

You therefore, my son, be strong in the grace that is in Christ Jesus. The things which you have heard from me in the presence of many witnesses, entrust these to faithful men who will be able to teach others also.
(2 Timothy 2:2)

As I am writing this book, it is an Olympic year. The Summer Games of 2016 are on the horizon. When the Olympics come around every four years, I am more interested in Track & Field and Swimming than anything else. Honestly, I am extremely *uninterested* in anything that requires a judge. I want the winners to be objective — throw or jump further and higher or cross the finish line first.

My favorite events — both on the track and in the pool — are the relay events. They are about more than speed and individual strengths. They are about teamwork, precision, and strategy. And the relays on the track have something that those in the pool do not have. They have the passing of the baton.

In the 2008 Summer Games in Beijing, both the U.S. men and women were highly favored to win the 4 X 100 meter relay events. Both teams failed. Why? Both teams dropped the baton.

Listen again to the words of the Apostle Paul to Timothy in 2 Timothy 2:2. *"The things which you have heard from me in the presence of many witnesses, entrust these to faithful men who will be able to teach others also."*

"In the presence of many witnesses... faithful men." This is accountability. There is nothing kept in secret. There are standards of faithfulness.

The rest of the verse describes a relay. Paul says, in effect, *"You heard this from me. You share it with others, who will share it with others, who will share it with others..."* That relay has continued all the way through the centuries until someone shared the truth of the gospel with you and with me! Accountability is a reminder that we must strategically pass the baton from one person to the next, one generation to the next, and one culture to the next.

I don't want my generation to be the one that drops the baton!

Here's one more passage that speaks to mutual accountability:

And let us consider how to stimulate one another to love and good deeds, not forsaking our own assembling together, as is the habit of some, but encouraging one another; and all the more as you see the day drawing near.
(Hebrews 10:24-25)

Accountability is about stimulating one another. For what purpose? For the purpose of love and good deeds. For the purpose of meeting together regularly as a congregation for mutual encouragement. We need each other because all of us have times that we need our intentions to be re-stimulated.

Since I'm a native Texan, I have a particular fondness for the NIV translation of these verses:

And let us consider how we may spur one another on toward love and good deeds, not giving up meeting together, as some are in the habit of doing, but encouraging one another — and all the more as you see the Day approaching.

Cowboy up! Get on your spurs! The spur imagery is a reminder that, within this mutual accountability, sometimes we need an extra nudge to get us re-focused. The purpose of spurs for the cowboy is not to injure his horse, but to create a moment of discomfort that regains the horse's attention.

I have described accountability and encouragement this way: Sometimes it is a comforting and soothing pat on the back; sometimes it is a gentle and motivating kick in the seat of the pants! Always it is for the purpose of helping one another fulfill our purpose as Christ-followers living out the *Christ-life*.

That idea is a perfect segue into the third missing component.

Missing Support

The final missing crucial component that I want to mention is **support**. It may be somewhat difficult to determine the difference between accountability and support in terms of what it actually looks like. I suppose the distinction I would make is this: *accountability is relational* and *support is systemic*.

Support seeks to provide the necessary processes and systems to give traction to the mutual accountability that we have chosen. Support asks, "What do you need from me (or us) to help you succeed?" Support says, "Your growth — not your comfort — is my priority. I will ask the hard questions. I will push you and point out when you are making excuses. I will call for your best. And I will be there to pick you up and dust you off when you stumble and fall."

Two passages from Proverbs 27 come to mind for me as I consider what **support** looks like:

Better is open rebuke than love that is concealed. Faithful are the wounds of a friend, but deceitful are the kisses of an enemy.
(Proverbs 27:5-6)

Rebuke? Wounds? With friends like that ...

But think about it. Wouldn't you rather have someone in your life who is so committed to your success and growth — so firmly on your side — that they will tell you the truth even if it is painful? Or would you rather have someone who just tells you what you want to hear, so they can get something in return?

I have been known to get sleepy while driving. My wife has been known to whack me when I am sleepy while driving. Why does she do that? One reason is that she is not eager to die in a car wreck, but another reason is that **she loves me enough to cause me short-term pain to keep me from long-term disaster.**

When we have developed the kind of relationships in our small groups where mutual accountability can thrive, we will not be afraid of those faithful wounds that come from our friends. We may not like it at the moment, but we will know it comes from those who are **for** us.

Iron sharpens iron, so one man sharpens another.
(Proverbs 27:17)

Do you know how iron sharpens iron? Intense contact. Friction. Sometimes so intense that some sparks fly. Those who won't get close enough to make contact can't sharpen us. Those who will only polish us, as with a soft cloth, can't sharpen us. That's not a support system; it's a flatter-fest. (I think I just made up another word).

Rodney Cox is the founder of Ministry Insights.[13] I have been through his training and consider Rodney a friend and brother in the Lord. I have heard him say more than once, "If what you have always believed were not really true, wouldn't you want to know it?"

Our initial response to that may be, "No! Don't tell me! My mistaken notions have served me just fine up until now!" But have they really?

In 1982, I was part of a group of college students who took a Spring Break mission trip to St. George, Utah. At the end of the week, we were traveling through Nevada on the way back home to Texas. We had 17 people traveling in a 15-passenger van. (We were, after all, college students). For reasons I still don't understand, we picked up a hitchhiker. (Perhaps we just weren't quite feeling cramped enough).

Several hours later, on a really dark stretch of highway, we passed a sign that said, "Welcome to California."

Just in case you are geographically challenged, I should point out that the shortest distance from Nevada to Texas does not include any part of California!

I remember two comments as we passed the sign...

Van driver (a fellow student): "What the heck are we doing in California?"

Hitchhiker: "I knew you missed a turn about an hour ago."

---

[13] Ministry Insights exists to provide Biblically based products and processes that help believers develop Christ-centered relationships. (ministryinsights.com)

He was not our friend.

He was also not on the van much longer, but that is another story. My point is that he was along for the ride. Our success was not his priority. As a result, he felt no compulsion to point out that we had missed our turn and had extended, by several hours, our sardine-can trip home.

In groups where every person's mission to live out the *Christ-life* is approached with *intentionality*, where relationships of mutual *accountability* are nurtured, and where systems and processes of *support* are put into place, **no one is just along for the ride**.

RECAP - Intentionality, Accountability, and Support in Group Bible Study

So, what does all this look like in practice? How does understanding these concepts help us truly make a difference in the effectiveness of our Bible study groups? Let me "bottom line" it for you.

Intentionality - Every member of the group understands that the #1 purpose of this group is to assist and encourage one another toward growth in living out the *Christ-life*. Everything we do will be centered on that goal.

Accountability - Every member of the group will leave every group meeting with a *specific action plan* for applying what we learned today and we will share those plans with one another so that we can be praying for one another during the week.

Support - We will report back to one another at each gathering how we did with our action plans from the previous gathering. We will celebrate victories. We will give the proper encouragement to those who struggle and help them process ways to approach the week ahead. We won't focus so much on what is *wrong*, but on what is *missing*.

The first three chapters have reinforced five spiritual health benefits of Bible study, looked at Jesus's plans for how we develop a spiritually healthy community, and identified three missing crucial components that contribute to the disconnect between Jesus's plans and our reality.

Now, the fun begins! Next, we are going to talk about how we create the kind of atmosphere and focus that can rescue the study of God's word from "Eat your vegetables Bible study" and transform it into a powerfully effective tool for disciple making.

Chapter 4 - Transforming "Bible Study" into Disciple Making

Imagine yourself in the waiting lounge of a five-star restaurant. You didn't just drop by this place on your way home. You've been planning it for a week. You made a reservation with some of your closest friends and turned down any request that would have interrupted this scheduled dinner. You built time into your schedule so that you could shower, shave, and shine and make the journey to the restaurant at a comfortable pace. You are already anticipating a fantastic dining experience and — even though you have not yet entered the dining room — you begin to salivate at the thought of the meal you are going to savor.

You enter the dining room and find that everything has been prepared with meticulous attention to detail. From the table settings to the menu, the noise level to the view — every consideration has been made to provide an exquisite dining experience. You enjoy the conversation with your friends as you peruse the menu. You have no doubt that the chef will deliver a perfectly prepared meal.

Your plates arrive and you see vegetables. But these vegetables are not just any vegetables. They are fresh, from farm to table. They are seasoned and cooked to perfection. They are so delectable that you can't help talking about them with your dinner companions. In fact, you are so amazed that you want to try preparing these vegetables at home.

The next day at work, you tell your coworkers about your dining experience. You don't just tell them about the food, you tell them about the whole experience and you invite them to join you for a future meal.

Now, that is how you serve vegetables!

I think by now I have made it clear that I believe that small groups that study the Bible together are important to the church, but that these small group "Bible studies" do not guarantee discipleship. It has been my intent, through the first three chapters, to emphasize the importance of studying God's word together, the framework of a Jesus-centered church, and the missing components of the typical group "Bible study" that keep discipleship from being nourished.

It is my intent in this chapter to move us from *eating more vegetables*, to *savoring together a balanced, well-prepared, and delicious spiritual meal that strengthens us for healthy living*.

10 Commandments of powerfully effective small group Bible study

Long before David Letterman made the "Top 10 List" famous, God gave His own top 10 list through Moses (Exodus 20). The 10 Commandments are practical and foundational life principles which, when properly applied, can result in success in living a powerfully effective life that honors God.

I want to use that framework to talk about 10 Commandments of powerfully effective small group Bible study — the kind of study that leads to real discipleship.

Before I get to those "commandments," I need you to notice three things.

First, these "commandments" are not found in the Bible. They are not un-Biblical or anti-Biblical, but they are non-Biblical, meaning that you won't find them explicitly stated in Scripture, nor should they be chiseled onto stone tablets. They should not be seen as "rules," but as "best practices." I'm just using the familiar metaphor of 10 Commandments.

Second, notice I call them "10 Commandments," not "THE 10 Commandments." These are just principles that I am suggesting and I limited the number to 10 to maintain the metaphor. There could be many more.

Third, just for fun, I went with King James English in stating these "commandments" and then followed each with a "Be" statement.

So, with those clarifications, we're ready to go. Can you hear the thunder? Just kidding.

1. Thou shalt not bore thy class.

Seriously. I'm not kidding. Nothing takes the winds out of the sails of a group Bible study quicker than a boring atmosphere. May I tell you a secret? If group Bible study is boring, it is not the Bible's fault! Think of what the Bible includes: romance, adventure, intrigue, flawed heroes, conquest, miracles, villains, ordinary people who experience the extraordinary, life lessons, purpose, glimpses into eternity, history, secrets to knowing God. How could that ever be boring!

No, boring group Bible study is not a result of a boring Bible, but a boring group study atmosphere.

The first time I taught this material in a church, I asked them to give me examples of what made group Bible study boring. The list was really short. Almost every person gave the same answer: **lecture.**

Why is lecture so boring? Because it only involves the teacher. It is monologue, not dialogue. It really doesn't cause group members to think and process. They can agree with what's being said or they can disagree with what's being said, but there is only one person making a contribution to the learning. Though we would never say this out loud, the implication is that only one person brings value to the lesson.

So if lecture is the number one reason why group Bible study is boring, then why is it still the most widely used method? Because it is the easiest to prepare. The teacher studies the lesson, prepares his or her remarks, shows up and teaches. (Or in some classes I have attended, the teacher looks over the lesson and then reads it in class out of the book. That, however, is not boring; it's lazy.)

May I offer an alternative? How much life could be brought into our group Bible studies if we scuttled the lecture method in favor of an **engaging discussion**? I know the pushback on this. I've heard it. *"I can't get anyone in my class to talk." "If I let people discuss, we will chase too many rabbits and I won't be able to get through the material."*

So, what is the main purpose of small group Bible study? Is it to get through the material or to engage people in the life changing and transformational study of God's word together? Answering this question may be the most powerful step you can take in transforming "Bible study" into disciple making.

If getting through the material is the ultimate goal, the group is unnecessary. If getting through the material is the ultimate goal, give them good material to read and send it home with them.

Here's my top reason why engaging people in the study of God's word together is more valuable than getting through the material: *faith is to be lived out in community*. Community means variety. Community means that every person's perspective is valuable. Community means that we are on a journey together. Community means we all have questions. Community means we have a safe place to ask our questions, express our perspectives, and learn from one another.

So, to choose engaging discussion over lecture means that teachers become discussion facilitators and need to develop a couple of skills.

The first skill is knowing how to ask questions.

We all know how to ask questions, right? You just kind of lift the pitch of your voice at the end of the last word to give the auditory signal of a question mark. I've noticed that some people have the irritating habit of making every statement sound like a question with that little raised pitch at the end of the sentence.

Here's the secret to asking questions: *you have to be seeking to gain something new through someone else's answer*. It may be a new insight, new information, or new perspective. The best and most powerful kinds of questions are open ones, rather than closed statements or rhetorical questions.

Val Hastings, founder of Coaching4Clergy[14], says,

"Powerful questions are usually open-ended, leaving room for contemplation and reflection, instead of being limited to yes or no or specific choices. Powerful questions promote the exploration of new possibilities and stimulate creativity... Limiting questions, on the other hand, might not be questions at all. They may only be thinly masking a statement of blame, obligation of guilt... [15]

Good question: *"When you think of _____, what comes to mind for you?"* This is open and calls for reflection.

Not so good question: *"When the Apostle Paul said _____, what did he mean?"* This seems like a rhetorical or trick question. It doesn't invite response because people may be afraid of giving the wrong answer. An alternative question might be, *"What applications can you think of for this statement from the Apostle Paul?"* Or *"If you could ask Paul to clarify his meaning, what question would you have?"*

Not so good question: *"Do you think that this is true?"* This doesn't call for anything but a yes/no answer. It may also seem like a trick question. An alternative question might be, *"What do you think about this?"* or *"If this were true, what is one thing that would mean for us today?"*

Terrible question: *"Why in the world would you think that?"* Do I really need to explain why this is a terrible

---

[14] coaching4clergy.com
[15] J. Val Hastings, *The Next Great Awakening: How to Empower God's People with a Coach Approach to Ministry*, 2010, Coaching4Clergy.

question? Okay — just in case — I will. It is not really a question. It is a statement. An alternative question might be, *"What led you to that conclusion?"* or *"I had not thought about it that way. Tell me more."*[16]

The second skill is to develop a healthy curiosity.

You won't ask good questions if you are not really curious about what people think. If you would rather get through the materials and make sure all the points of the "lesson" are made, then don't ask questions just because someone suggested that you should try to get the class talking. People are smart enough to figure out if you are really curious or not.

Bottom Line: BE ENGAGING

2. Thou shalt celebrate authenticity.

I'm not sure when the phrase "***keeping it real***" came into vogue. I'm not even sure I know what that means, but **real** seems to be what a whole lot of people are concerned about keeping **it** (whatever **it** is).

Here's what I *am* sure about: Every person has a story. Each one has a past that influences, informs, and sometimes even imprisons them in various ways. Each one has a present that consumes most of their energy and attention. Each one has a future that may frighten or excite them, depending on the day. Some days it may be both.

---

[16] I have included a list of a few more possible questions in Appendix 1.

They bring those stories with them to your group.

Is your group a safe place to share those stories? Is taking off the masks permitted and even encouraged? Are fears, doubts, and anxieties just as welcome as victories and celebrations? Will this group walk together through the messiness that sometimes constitutes the journey we call *living*?

Those are real questions that, more than likely, no one will ever ask out loud. They might not even think through them, but they are basic to a sense of belonging. Most people are really, really tired of faking their way through life, pretending that they have a handle on everything so they won't be rejected, and having many acquaintances, but too few real friends.

So, how do you, as a group leader, achieve this kind of authenticity? You can't. It cannot be achieved, manufactured, or announced. *"So, today, dear group members, we are going to get real with one another. From now on, we are going to experience authenticity in our group."*

I'm pretty sure that kind of announcement would not have the desired outcome, unless the desired outcome is scaring some people out of their wits and opening the door for the completely self-absorbed and emotionally needy people to turn the group time into their own personal therapy session.

No, this authenticity can only be experienced, celebrated, and encouraged. It is not an atmosphere that tries to *force* the stories to the surface, but allows them to surface naturally out of a desire to see how God is moving in lives, how His word speaks to real circumstances, and how having close companions can multiply our effectiveness on the journey of the **Christ-life**.

Bear one another's burdens, and thereby fulfill the law of Christ.
(Galatians 6:2)

Bottom Line: BE REAL

3. Thou shalt prepare with intentionality.

There's that word again. **Intentionality.** Yes, I have to admit that it is one of my favorite words. I'm a big fan of being strategic and purposeful in everything I do. Sometimes I even *do nothing* on purpose.

Have you ever attended a meeting where it was obvious that little or no preparation had gone into it and those in charge were simply "*winging it?*"

I am often the guest preacher in small churches. I could write a whole book on crazy or, at the very least, quirky things I've seen these churches do. One of the most interesting ones I remember was the time that they spent the first few minutes doing the following:

1. Deciding who would play the piano today.
2. Deciding who would lead the singing today.
3. Talking about what songs both song leader and piano player knew.

I should point out that these things happened *after* the service had started, *while* the congregation sat and watched.

I've also been in far too many Sunday School classes where it was obvious that the only preparation anyone put into it was getting up, getting dressed, and driving to the church building.

Full disclosure also requires that I admit that I have come ill prepared both as a leader and as a participant. Full disclosure also requires that I admit that very little of value *ever* happened when I came that way.

So, how can a group leader prepare with intentionality? I'm going to suggest four different kinds of necessary preparation.

The first is **spiritual preparation**. Spiritual preparation is not a hasty prayer asking God to "be with us" as we study. Spiritual preparation isn't getting up early on Sunday to look through and pray over the lesson one last time.

Spiritual preparation is ongoing. **It is a life of prayer and consistently walking with God.** It is living out the **Christ-life** seven days a week so that when you gather with your group, you are leading out of an abundant spirituality. It doesn't mean that you will not sometimes be less than your best. It means that you have tapped into a renewable source of spiritual vitality.

But those who trust in the Lord will find new strength. They will soar high on wings like eagles. They will run and not grow weary. They will walk and not faint.
(Isaiah 40:31, NLT)

The second preparation is **mental**. Here's where you think deeply about the purpose of this group session. Here's where you make the time to thoroughly prepare the lesson, gaining a thorough understanding of both the *Biblical text* to be discussed *and* the *desired outcomes* in the lives of the group members.

Part of the mental preparation is identifying and crafting two or three of those *powerful questions* that were referenced in the first commandment. Rather than waiting to see what questions pop into your head on the spur of the moment, or using the same questions every time the group meets, prepare questions that will open up dialogue around this particular passage of Scripture or topic of discussion.

The third preparation is **emotional**. This is where you bring your heart to this lesson. What's *your* story? How do *you* connect with this passage or topic? How does this lesson comfort you? Convict you? Challenge you? Encourage you?

As the leader, your sharing of your heart connection to this passage or topic models authenticity and helps nurture the atmosphere where it is safe for others to share their heart connection and allow their own stories to bubble up to the surface.

The final preparation I want to mention is **physical**. It is my opinion that this one is the most neglected and yet the easiest to do, because it can be facilitated through a clear **three-part routine**. I am going to use a typical Sunday morning on-campus Bible study for the example, but I think the principles are true regardless of location and the routine can be tweaked as necessary.

Part one: get a good night's sleep the night before. You will not — I repeat, *will not* — bring the best of you to your Sunday morning Bible study if you are up late on Saturday night! It doesn't matter whether you stay *out* late or just stay *up* late; it affects you more than you realize.

I made a choice many years ago to very, very rarely accept any invitations for things that happened on Saturday evening. That was an intentional choice to do everything possible to be at my best for Sunday morning.[17]

Part two: get up early enough on Sunday morning to avoid having to rush. I know you are really sharp. You are proving that by reading this book. You are so sharp that you will notice how part one and part two go hand in hand. To be able to get up early on Sunday morning to avoid having to rush, you have to go to bed early enough to get a good night's sleep. Mind. Boggling.

I like to be up, drinking coffee and spending *personal* time with Jesus, at least two hours before I have to go anywhere. As crazy as it seems, that is even more important for me on the day when I am going to be spending extended *group* time with Jesus. An un-rushed morning at home leads to an uncluttered and un-frazzled mind and spirit once I arrive at the place of worship, study, and fellowship.

Part three: arrive early enough at the location of the Bible study to prepare the space. Sometimes there are tables and chairs to get ready. Sometimes there's a pot of coffee to be made. Sometimes there is a need to make sure any supplies, handouts, or visuals are ready before group members start arriving.

Why *before* they start arriving? What's a better use of the time once they get there — gathering stuff and moving furniture or having relationship-building conversations? That seems like a no-brainer to me.

---

[17] I have included some tips for a good night's sleep in Appendix 2.

Bottom Line: BE PREPARED

4. Thou shalt redeem the time.

*See then that ye walk circumspectly, not as fools, but as wise, **redeeming the time**, because the days are evil.*
(Ephesians 5:15-16, KJV emphasis added)

*Therefore be careful how you walk, not as unwise men but as wise, **making the most of your time**, because the days are evil.*
(NASB)

So, how do you **make the most of your time**, with reference to group Bible study?

First, recognize that time is not unlimited. You have a certain amount of time to accomplish a certain purpose. Wow! No pressure! Actually, it should not make you feel pressured. It should excite you that you have this window of opportunity to do something of eternal significance. It should make you want to rise to the challenge and bring your "A" game every time. It is the opening bell! It is the tip off! It's game time!

Secondly, it helps to know that, in the language of the New Testament, there are two different words/concepts of time, and both of them need to be maximized.

The first word is *chronos* and it is the word from which we get our English word *chronology*. I like to refer to it as **clock time**. The second word is *kairos*. I like to refer to it as **appropriate time**. What's the distinction? Think of it this way:

It's 12:00. Time for lunch. That's *chronos* time. It is time to have lunch because we have lunch when the clock says it is time for lunch.

I'm hungry. Let's get some lunch. That's *kairos* time. The clock may say it is 10:45 or 1:30, but it is time to have lunch because we are ready to eat.

That's really simplified, but I think it makes the point. So, what does that mean for our groups?

Maximizing the *chronos* time looks like this: Do you start and stop on time? Do you arrive early enough that you can do so? If your group meets before the worship service, do your group members have adequate time to go to the restroom, pick up their kids, and make it into the worship service in time to find a seat?

Because of the nature of my current ministry, I don't attend "Sunday School" very often. But I did almost every Sunday for most of my life. The vast majority of the classes I attended in the past, and sometimes attend now, NEVER started on time as far as the clock is concerned. If Sunday School starts at 10:00, it is a rare occasion for anything to actually happen before 10:15 (other than "fellowship"... which is a much nicer word than "gossip").

Do you know why these groups don't start on time? Because most of the members of the group don't arrive on time. They trickle in for that first 10-15 minutes. And may I let you in on a dirty little church secret? ***The members don't arrive on time because we have trained them to be late!*** They know that there is no reason to be on time because they know we won't start on time. No matter what time they have ever arrived, they have never found the group discussion/lesson already in session.

Then the snowball effect happens. The people who do arrive on time start to get frustrated because we don't start on time. So, they start showing up later. The class session gets started later... and the discussion is either rushed or cut short because we are running out of time... and so we stop later... and we have to rush to the worship service... and the worship service begins to start later because people are slowly trickling in... and the people who are on time start realizing the worship service is going to start later... and so they start showing up later...

Chronos time matters, friends! Does that seem a little dramatic? Maybe, but there's a lot more truth there than we would like to admit.

What about *kairos* time? How do we maximize that? No, ignoring the clock is not the answer! *Chronos* time asks, "What time is it on the *clock*?" *Kairos* time asks, "What time is it in the *world*?"

That's not about different time zones (that would be still be *chronos*); it is about world events, cultural conditions, issues that have people thinking and talking. It is about bringing the truth of Scripture to bear on what is happening in the world and processing together how we live out the **Christ-life** in our culture.[18]

Kairos time also asks, "What time is it in the *lives of our group members*?" What's going on with them? What are their struggles? What's happening in their families? What are their fears? What are they excited about? How are we

---

[18] I talk more in depth about how we respond to the culture in my book, *Culture Wars: In Search of Spiritual Jedi*. More information at drgerrylewis.com/culturewars.

encouraging each other to live out the **Christ-life** at home, at work, and at school?

What an amazing opportunity we have when we are gathered! Next week's *kairos* time will be different. We have *this moment* to speak into this point in time.

Bottom Line: BE TIMELY

5. Thou shalt engage THE STORY.

How many possible Bible passages could we study together in our groups? Well, there are 1189 chapters. Verses are a little harder to count due to the variety within translations, but there are over 31,000. How many Bible stories? Hundreds.

But there is really one grand story that encompasses every other. It is the story of God's activity in the world as recorded in both Old and New Testaments. It is **THE STORY** and it has one main character: Jesus!

The Old Testament points to God's ultimate self-revelation in Christ.

> *In the past God spoke to our ancestors through the prophets at many times and in various ways, but in these last days **he has spoken to us by his Son**, whom he appointed heir of all things, and through whom also he made the universe. The **Son is the radiance of God's glory and the exact representation of his being**, sustaining all things by his powerful word.*
> (Hebrews 1:1-3, NIV emphasis added)

No matter what today's text, our intent is to grow in grace and knowledge of the Lord Jesus Christ and to bring the text studied to bear on how we are living out the **Christ-life**. We must never isolate ourselves or our stories from **THE STORY**.

Bottom Line: BE FOCUSED

6. Thou shalt embrace the mission of the church.

Back in Chapter 2, I stated my firm conviction that every church has the same purpose for existing: **to glorify God and make disciples**. If this is not our purpose, we are spinning our wheels and both my time writing and your time reading this book would be better spent doing something else. That's how much I am convinced!

But I also believe that every congregation has a unique mission within their context. In *Church Unique*, Will Mancini uses the term *"Kingdom Concept: We will glorify God and make disciples by _____."*

Out of that Kingdom Concept is derived the church's unique mission and vision. The Church Unique process helps walk a church through developing that mission and vision, along with values, strategies, and measures.[19]

I am not certified to implement a Church Unique process in churches, but I am familiar enough with the concepts that I am able to use them — along with other resources — as discussion points in helping churches develop their mission and vision. I do need to be clear, however, that I'm not talking about a "mission statement" as much as I am talking about a "statement of our mission."

---

[19] For more information on the Church Unique process see auxano.com.

That sounds like a consultant, doesn't it? Just rearrange the words and call it new! The invoice for my consultant fee is in the mail.

No, it is not that simple. There really is a difference. Let me explain.

So often, when churches develop a "mission statement," they start with the *statement*. The leaders get together (or the pastor does it alone) and compose the statement. They will use general Biblical concepts (*Love God, Share the Good News, Exalt Jesus, etc.*) or adapt statements from other churches (*Help people become fully devoted followers of Christ, Impact our community with the Gospel, etc.*). They will make banners, signs, logos, and start trying to infuse the "mission statement" into the life of the church.

Please note: I am not suggesting that these are bad mission statements or that these churches are doing it all wrong.

I am suggesting that there is a difference between:

1. Starting with a well crafted "mission statement" and hoping that our congregation will understand and embrace it.

   OR

2. Processing together our **Who** (the congregation that God has brought together), our **Where** (the context in which God has placed us), and our **Why** (the driving passion with which God has already captured us) and then finding a way to state it in a way that is clear, concise, and compelling.

The first option starts with the *statement*. The second starts with the *mission*. People tend to not get overly excited about "mission statements." But if they have clarity on what the "mission" is and it is stated in a compelling way, then there is something on which to build momentum.

Since this book is about disciple making and group Bible study, I won't unpack that any further. But I thought clarity on the concept necessary to explain what I mean by **"embrace the mission of the church"** in our Bible study groups. There are three parts to this.

The first is to **know the mission** of the church. Of course, that can't *originate* in a Bible study group. If the church as a whole is not clear on its compelling mission, then it will be difficult for groups to embrace it. However, it could *initiate* in a Bible study group. How cool would it be for a Bible study group to go to church leaders and say, *"We want to help our church fulfill its mission. How can we do that?"*

For the sake of this discussion, let's say the church has a statement of mission that is known. Simply knowing the mission is not enough. The second part is where **embrace the mission** comes in. Your group can know the church's mission and still choose to operate with its own agenda. I'm not sure anyone would say this out loud (though it wouldn't shock me), but the group could say, *"We know the church's mission is _____, but OUR mission is _____."*

Here's what that statement — either spoken aloud or simply acted out in practice — says: *We are our own church! We will participate with the rest of the church as it suits us. We will expect access to all church resources to help us fulfill our own purposes, but we do not see it as our responsibility to be an integral part of helping the church fulfill its mission.*

I have seen this attitude played out in so many ways in churches. A group wants to select their own study materials without any consideration of how those materials may or may not support the current direction of the church. A group stakes their claim on a particular room in the church with no consideration of helping the church use limited space most effectively.

I am not suggesting that a group should have no say in the choice of study materials or in decorating and setting up their meeting space. I'm saying that it shouldn't be done in isolation, forgetting that all those "*one another*" passages relate to the whole church, not just our group. ***Our group does not have its own mission; we are an integral part of helping our church fulfill its mission.***

The third part of this is **connecting the dots within the mission.** Not only is our group an integral part of helping our church fulfill its mission; we are partners with every other ministry in doing so. Bible study, worship, missions, ministry, and outreach — all of these are interdependent and connected in fulfilling the mission of the church. Each of these has its own *role.* None of these has its own *mission.*

For even as the body is one and yet has many members, and all the members of the body, though they are many, are one body, so also is Christ. For by one Spirit we were all baptized into one body, whether Jews or Greeks, whether slaves or free, and we were all made to drink of one Spirit.

For the body is not one member, but many. If the foot says, "Because I am not a hand, I am not a part of the body," it is not for this reason any the less a part of the body. And if the ear says, "Because I am not an eye, I am not a part of the body," it is not for this reason any the less a part of the body. If the whole body were an eye, where would the hearing be? If the whole were hearing, where would the sense of smell be? But now God has placed the members, each one of them, in the body, just as He desired. If they were all one member, where would the body be?

But now there are many members, but one body. And the eye cannot say to the hand, "I have no need of you;" or again the head to the feet, "I have no need of you." On the contrary, it is much truer that the members of the body which seem to be weaker are necessary; and those members of the body which we deem less honorable, on these we bestow more abundant honor, and our less presentable members become much more presentable, whereas our more presentable members have no need of it. But God has so composed the body, giving more abundant honor to that member which lacked, so that there may be no division in the body, but that the members may have the same care for one another. And if one member suffers, all the members suffer with it; if one member is honored, all the members rejoice with it. Now you are Christ's body, and individually members of it.
(1 Corinthians 12:12-27)

Bottom Line: BE ON MISSION

7. Thou shalt encourage the Body.

That passage from 1 Corinthians 12 is a perfect segue into this commandment. Probably the three most commonly used Biblical metaphors for the Church are: The Bride of Christ, The Family of God, and The Body of Christ. All of them are good and completely Biblical and emphasize a particular aspect of the Church's role in the world. To leave any one of them out is to give an incomplete representation. However, the Body of Christ is my personal favorite.

I personally resonate with the Body metaphor. It is less likely to be filtered through modern Western structures than the Bride and Family metaphors. When we start trying to identify bridesmaids, stepchildren, and ex-mothers-in-law to make the metaphors work, that is just confusing!

It is, however, easy to explain that the body is the visible representation of the real person. When someone sees my body — such as it is — that's what they identify as Gerry. There are things about me they can't see (thoughts, passions, preferences, spiritual realities, and the like). It could be argued that those things are the real me, but they can only be seen as they show up through the visible representation that is this middle-aged, white, male body.

For some reason that I don't understand, God has chosen to present the church as **the Body of Christ - the visible representation of Jesus in the world**. And I believe "**being the Body**" is an infinitely more compelling purpose than "**doing church.**"

Being the body means that we are doing life together. We are a family in the best sense of the word. We are an interconnected and interdependent community, living out the **Christ-life** together. We don't just gather for an hour or two each week and then go and live our separate, disconnected lives. We belong *with* and *to* each other. We are *for* each other.

Our small group Bible studies can and should be powerful tools for the purpose of enabling us to live out the **Christ-life** in community. According to Thom Rainer, President and CEO of Lifeway Christian Resources[20], people who get connected in a small group are five times more likely to assimilate into the body life of the church than those who only attend worship services.

Five. Times.

If that small group is intentionally focused on making disciples, and they are constantly seeking to draw new members into their group — and, by extension, the larger body of the church — can you see how powerful that is?

Bottom Line: BE CONNECTED

8. Thou shalt empower disciples.

If the purpose of the church is to glorify God and make disciples, and our small group is interconnected and interdependent with the larger body, and we are an integral part of helping our church fulfill its mission, then the purpose of our small group Bible study is to glorify God and make disciples. But, I'll go a step further.

It is our purpose to glorify God through empowering disciples who make disciples.

---

[20] lifeway.com

94

For that reason, I prefer saying that we have a *disciple making process*, rather than a *discipleship program*. Remember 2 Timothy 2:2?

You have heard me teach things that have been confirmed by many reliable witnesses. Now teach these truths to other trustworthy people who will be able to pass them on to others.
(NLT)

That empowering disciple making process is created through the *intentionality*, *accountability*, and *support* I talked about in Chapter 3. Our goal is that no one passes through our group without being empowered for their own journey on the **Christ-life** and equipped to be an empowering force for others on their journey.

Bottom Line: BE PURPOSEFUL

9. Thou shalt unleash ministers.

Who are the ministers in your church? I'm not asking the names or positions of your church staff. I'm asking who is called to ministry.

Here's another passage from 1 Corinthians 12:

*Now there are varieties of gifts, but the same Spirit. And there are varieties of ministries, and the same Lord. There are varieties of effects, but **the same God who works all things in all persons**. But **to each one** is given the manifestation of the Spirit for the common good. For to one is given the word of wisdom through the Spirit, and to another the word of knowledge according to the same Spirit; to another faith by the same Spirit, and to another gifts of healing by the one Spirit, and to another the*

*effecting of miracles, and to another prophecy, and to another the distinguishing of spirits, to another various kinds of tongues, and to another the interpretation of tongues. But one and the same Spirit works all these things, distributing **to each one individually** just as He wills.*
(1 Corinthians 12:4-11, emphasis added)

Take a look at this one as well:

*Therefore I, the prisoner of the Lord, implore you to walk in a manner worthy of **the calling with which you have been called**, with all humility and gentleness, with patience, showing tolerance for one another in love, being diligent to preserve the unity of the Spirit in the bond of peace. There is one body and one Spirit, **just as also you were called** in one hope of your calling; one Lord, one faith, one baptism, one God and Father of all who is over all and through all and in all. But **to each one of us** grace was given according to the measure of Christ's gift.*
(Ephesians 4:1-7, emphasis added)

There really is no simpler way to say this: ***Every Christ-follower is called to ministry***. To be on mission to live out the ***Christ-life*** is to be in ministry. A person's ministry may be carried out primarily through the church or it may be carried out primarily in a non-church workplace. It may even be carried out primarily at home, but *if you are following Jesus, you are called to ministry*.

One of the tasks of the church in empowering disciples is to help people find their ministry. We do that through helping them discover how God has uniquely wired them with personality, spiritual gifts, strengths, passions, and how He has equipped them through life experiences.[21]

Once we have helped people with the self-discovery part, the next step is to provide them opportunities to put those gifts, strengths, and passions into use in hands-on ministry. We provide them with the necessary training, tools, accountability, and support to help them succeed. Finally, we empower them to soar by trusting them and unleashing them to fulfill their ministry.

This is going to sound like a contradiction of something I said earlier, but stick with me. The small group is a mini-church in this unleashing process. Didn't I say we are not our own church? That's the key. Our small group is not our *own separate and disconnected* church.

But we can be the church in microcosm. Within our group we can help people put their gifts, strengths, and passions into practice. We can demonstrate the expectation that every member has a ministry to fulfill. We can empower and unleash ministers that help our group fulfill *our* mission of helping the church fulfill *its* mission.

What do you call a church where only a handful of people are doing the work of ministry and the rest are casual observers? Some might say you call it normal. I'd say you call it a bad church model.

---

[21] Two of my favorite resources for this discovery process are P.L.A.C.E. Ministries (placeministries.org) and Ministry Insights (ministryinsights.com). I use both of these extensively in my work with churches and church leaders.

I'd also say that the most effective way to change that approach church-wide is not to try to adopt it church-wide. It is to begin with the small groups. A small group that has a teacher who is expected to teach, keep up with members, organize outreach and fellowship, and lead the group to do ministry — while most everyone else is simply a casual observer — is just a bad church model in micro!

But a small group where responsibilities and ministries are divided up according to the gifts, strengths, and passions of the members of the class and where people are empowered, mentored, and coached in discovering and fulfilling their calling — this is a place where the bad church model can begin to be replaced.

And I am convinced that a spark that happens within a small group can be fanned into a flame that ignites movement across a congregation.

Bottom Line: BE CATALYTIC

10. Thou shalt journey with joy.

I remember vividly a church experience from my early teens. The little Baptist church where we attended had scheduled "revival" services for a week. That was a part of our church life every year. A guest preacher and song leader would come and lead us in special services every night for a week, in the hopes that lost people would come to Jesus and Christians would be revived and stirred up to greater service.

This particular year, we had a guest preacher who told us all week how much he missed home and how he really wished he were not spending the week at our church. But

God sent him to us, and he was being obedient. At least that was what he said he was doing.

With over four decades of hindsight, I can say that what he was really doing was wasting our — and God's — time. I know you will find this to be shocking, but I don't recall anything positive from that week of revival. No one got revived or came to faith in Christ. Shocking, right?
I have another memory from the time when my kids were young teens. Our family went together as a part of a group mission trip to Mexico. In the church where we were working that week, the pastor's wife was absolutely amazing!

Here's what her days that week looked like. Get up in the morning and cook breakfast for her family. Travel to the church building for Vacation Bible School. Lead a rowdy group of more than 50 kids in singing and then teach them all a Bible story. Then, while the kids broke into smaller groups and did some arts and crafts, she worked on preparing the snacks that they would feed to each child to send them home with a full stomach.

After the kids went home, she served our group the lunch she had prepared for us. Then she got in the car with her husband and drove 90 miles one way to the facility where she was having chemotherapy treatments. After chemo, they would drive the 90 miles back home and rest for the evening. Then she would get up the next day and do the same thing again.

If I had one word to describe her, it would be *joyful*.

My friends, as those who are on this journey of the Christ-life — those who have been called by Jesus out of separation and darkness into fellowship and light and who have the indwelling presence of the Spirit of the living God and the promise of Heaven — we have more to be joyful about than anyone else for any other reason on the face of this planet!

I'm not talking about "terminal positivity" where you slap a smile on your face and pretend that life is all sunshine and daffodils. I'm talking about deep, abiding, purposeful, eternity-focused joy.

Rejoice in the Lord always; again I will say, rejoice! Let your gentle spirit be known to all men. The Lord is near. Be anxious for nothing, but in everything by prayer and supplication with thanksgiving let your requests be made known to God. And the peace of God, which surpasses all comprehension, will guard your hearts and your minds in Christ Jesus.

Finally, brethren, whatever is true, whatever is honorable, whatever is right, whatever is pure, whatever is lovely, whatever is of good repute, if there is any excellence and if anything worthy of praise, dwell on these things. The things you have learned and received and heard and seen in me, practice these things, and the God of peace will be with you.
(Philippians 4:4-9)

What kind of atmosphere exists in your Bible study group? Is it a forced positivity where every person feels like they need to put on their happy face and fake it through the time together? Is it a whine and complain session about the state of the world?

Or is it a place where real people, share real life together, encouraging one another through the reality that a very real God is right here with us?

Bottom Line: BE JOYFUL

RECAP – 10 commandments for transforming "Bible study"

1. Thou shalt not bore thy class (Be engaging).
2. Thou shalt celebrate authenticity (Be real).
3. Thou shalt prepare with intentionality (Be prepared).
4. Thou shalt redeem the time (Be timely).
5. Thou shalt engage THE STORY (Be focused).
6. Thou shalt embrace the mission of the church (Be on mission).
7. Thou shalt encourage the Body (Be connected).
8. Thou shalt empower disciples (Be purposeful).
9. Thou shalt unleash ministers (Be catalytic).
10. Thou shalt journey with joy (Be joyful).

Hopefully, by this point you are convinced that studying the Bible together in groups is important and you have seen that a focus and atmosphere that is different from the typical "Bible study" group is possible.

Next, I'm going to give you a couple of specific and practical tools that you can implement immediately to support the vision and transform it to reality.

Chapter 5 - Cleanup On the Bible Study Aisle!

One of the things that makes me a little crazy in both preaching and teaching is something that I have done just as poorly as anyone else — that is to be long on concepts, but short on application. I don't want to be guilty of that in this book.

I think everything I have written so far is true and important (otherwise I would not have written it). I think the concepts are sound and have the potential to impact disciple making processes in churches of all sizes and shapes.

But, I don't want to just share good concepts without sharing some practical, user-friendly methods that lend themselves toward solid application.

The S.O.A.P.Y. Method of Bible Study

In 2010, my friend Harrell Teague, from San Antonio Baptist Association, introduced me to a simple Bible study method they were using within their staff. He called it the **S.O.A.P.** method.[22]

Here's how I have chosen to unpack this concept:

---

[22] I don't know if SABA originated this method or borrowed it, but Harrell was the first person I heard it from.

S - Scripture. This is the Biblical text to be considered. Each person in the group reads and meditates on the passage, in advance of the group session. In response to their reading and meditation, group members record their...

O - Observations. What is this passage saying? What words or phrases stand out? What questions arise? What concepts and lessons are clarified? As observations are recorded, the next step is for each person to consider...

A - Application. How can the lessons here be put into practice? Each person asks, "What is a personal application that helps me live out the *Christ-life* this week?"

Group members do these three steps individually ahead of time. Then, when the group meets, they share their observations and applications with one another through open group discussion. This discussion then leads to...

P - Prayer. The group prays for one another and asks for guidance, grace, and strength to make the personal applications. The group also prays for one another's needs and concerns, but this method makes *prayer for our growth as disciples* a central and intentional component (that's part of the accountability and support).

I have added one more letter to this method.

Y - You. One of my favorite seminary professors, Dr. J.W. MacGorman, defined *faith* as "belief plus yourself." Adding *yourself* to the **S.O.A.P.** method raises the accountability and support quotient.

Here's what I mean — it is great to identify an application that I **can** make to grow in living out the *Christ-life* this week. It is a whole different matter to identify an action I *will* take in the next week, share it with the group, ask them to pray for me, and report back how it went when we gather the next time. Few motivations are more powerful than going public with an action plan. (As I write these words, I am 65 hours from the public deadline I posted to have completed the first draft of this manuscript. You can be sure that I am doing everything I can to make that happen!)[23]

I hope you can see that this method is simple without being simplistic, profound without being complicated, and scalable enough to be adapted to a variety of curricula. It could be used to study through a book of the Bible. It could just as easily be used in a topical study.

Give it a try in your Bible study group and let me know what happens.[24]

The 4 Question Method for Processing God's Word Together

Another simple, yet effective method for facilitating powerful group discussion is the **4 Question** method.[25] This method may be particularly effective if the curriculum being used is so detailed that the **S.O.A.P.Y.** method seems strained.

For this method, we need to allow enough time at the end of the study to ask these 4 questions and process them as a group:

----

[23] I finished with 60 hours to spare!

[24] Send me an email at contactgerrylewis@gmail.com.

[25] I honestly can't remember where I first heard this one.

1. **What did you like best about this study?** This question engages people at an emotional level.
2. **What did you not like or not understand?** This question engages people at both emotional and cognitive levels.
3. **What did you learn about God?** This question engages people cognitively and helps them reflect theologically (even if "theology" is a scary thought to them).
4. **What must we do?** This question engages people at the level of will, choice, and action as a follower of Jesus and provides accountability.

It is important to not give the impression that these questions are a "wrap up" to close the study. If group participants have that mindset, they will begin to shut down and disengage. This is not a *wrap up*, but a *workshop;* it is where the content of the Scripture becomes real in our lives.

The curriculum content is like reading a book on the health benefits of vegetables. The **4 questions** allow us to share our thoughts and recipes together in the kitchen, so we are better equipped for healthy living.

So, how much time should we allow for this group processing? My suggestion is *half the allotted time* for the study session. It is better to go deeper with less content than to stay shallow with more.

A word of caution

For any group leader who believes you can walk into the next session of your group and announce that you will be shifting to one or both of these methods — **DON'T DO IT!**

The old adage is true: ***the only person who really wants and likes change is a wet baby***.

These kinds of shifts are never accomplished through proclamations, only through positive experiences. To tell them you are going to be changing the style of their study is to invite resistance at best and opposition at worst.

It is far better to just begin introducing components of these methods by doing them. Start planting seeds by asking questions and nurturing the first little sprouts of dialogue and discussion that happen. Keep engaging your group until they begin experiencing consistent dynamic discussions and going deeper in their accountability and support. It is not necessary that the members of the group even know there is such thing as a **S.O.A.P.Y.** method or a **4 Question** method. They just need the benefits that come through experiencing these methods.

Epilogue - Yes, you can!

When I set out to write this book, I had two primary goals in mind:

1. To deliver some practical and effective content to church leaders and, specifically, to those who lead small group Bible studies.

2. To keep it short enough that busy group leaders would take the time to read it.

I hope I have succeeded on both counts. But, I also know how many times I have learned something new — either through reading or attending a workshop of some kind — and have brought it back to my church, only to have the "cold water committee" dump on it with those dreaded words, *"We've never done it that way before. It won't work here."*

Don't despair. It *will* work here.

Change doesn't happen overnight. It took a while for your group — or all the groups in your church — to arrive at the present state and it will take a while to get to the place where God wants you to be. One of the challenges of all leaders (including the one writing this) is getting things pointed in the right direction and celebrating every positive step. We want to go from point **A** to point **Z** — today if possible! And if not today, certainly by next week!

Take me out to the (church) ballgame

Who doesn't enjoy a day at the ballpark? Who doesn't get excited when the home team knocks it out of the park?

Just like baseball fans love home runs, so do churches. I'm sure you've heard parishioners say things like:

> *"Boy, the pastor hit a home run with that sermon!"*

> *"That outreach event was a home run!"*

> *"Our services have been a little dry lately. We really need to knock it out of the park this week."* (Ouch!)

Sometimes we act like only home runs matter. Why would we ever be satisfied with a little old single when we should be swinging for the fences? Don't we value excellence?

Yet, as I ponder the similarities between baseball and church life, three questions come to mind:

1. Why are we always looking for home runs in the form of exciting events or evangelistic "extravaganzas?"

That's easy. "Roundtrippers" are exciting and dramatic. When I attend a game at Globe Life Park in Arlington, a Texas Rangers' home run sparks fireworks, loud music, and deafening cheers. With one swing, everything can change. In just seconds, a grand slam can transform a three-run deficit into a one-run lead and shift momentum.

That's why homers are so addictive — and so dangerous. The batter that loses perspective can swing for the fences every time and wind up often striking out. Compare Major League Baseball's all-time home run leaders and all-time strikeout leaders; you will find a lot of the same names on both lists.

As a longtime Rangers fan, it's painful to recall them leading the league in home runs four of five years from 2001 to 2005 and not coming close to the playoffs. Winning a home run title is little consolation for a losing season.

2. What are the benefits of a base hit?

A base hit may not create the same adrenaline rush, but it keeps the team moving forward. If a team can string enough base hits together, it is going to score. Keep hitting and scoring, and it wins.

The church that is continually engaging with and serving its community and demonstrating the love of Christ — despite a lack of visible excitement — is like a steady hitter. The leaders in batting average, runs batted in, and on-base percentage are usually not power hitters. They just continue "making contact."

Here's a truth you can take to the bank: the team with the most home runs is not guaranteed a win, but the team that scores the most runs always wins.

3. So, what are the implications for the church?

A base hit represents the *power of incremental change*. We often fail to meet church goals because we try to get from point **A** to point **Z** instead of from **A** to **B** and then **C**. A base hit is a reminder that small victories have a cumulative effect and create momentum.

A base hit is also a powerful reminder of the *encouraging culture of celebration*. If we only celebrate home runs, we will fail to encourage and empower those who are "making contact" and moving forward daily.

A base hit also minimizes the focus on "me" and recognizes the *synergy of "we."* It is a visible witness of the "body" metaphors in 1 Corinthians 12 and Romans 12. After all, the only "Hall-of-Famer" in the Body is the Head. The rest of us need each other to serve His purposes.

This leaves the most important questions: **What was the last base hit your church celebrated? How will you encourage the next one?**
The One Class (or One Group) Attitude

We all want our whole church to embrace powerful transforming processes. As a leader of a regional network, I want every church to embrace powerful transforming processes. Those are not bad goals, but it is like moving from point **A** to point **Z** — not highly likely.

A great — and completely realistic — base hit would be to focus on one group that will say, *"As for me and my group/class, we will make disciples."*[26] One group, one focus: disciple making. There will be no casual observers. No one will be along for the ride.

Likely, this will need to come about through formation of a new group. It is easier to start something new with an intentional focus than it is to try to refocus an existing group. Every person who is a part of this group knows that the goal is for them to eventually leave this group equipped to help start another one.

---

[26] *"As for me and my house, we will serve the Lord."* (Joshua 24:15)

Starting this group may mean shifting the best leaders/disciplers from existing groups. Doing such a thing will result in some push back. People will accuse you of playing favorites.

Howard Hendricks taught for over 60 years at Dallas Theological Seminary, impacting the lives of more than 13,000 students during his tenure. Many of those students remember him for his famous quotes. Some that apply here are:

"If you cannot be accused of exclusivity, you are not discipling."

"Nothing is more common than unfulfilled potential."
"You teach what you know, but you reproduce what you are."

"Spend the rest of your life doing what God prepared you to do."

"You never graduate from the school of discipleship."

He also said, *"It is a sin to bore people with the Bible."* I never had the pleasure of studying under Prof Hendricks, but maybe he would approve of my first commandment from Chapter 4 - *Thou shall not bore thy class.*

So, what will it cost you to decide that disciple making must become the priority of your small group ministry? What will it cost you to take the first step toward seeing that vision become a reality?

What is it costing you not to?

I'm praying that every pastor, church leader, and group leader who reads this book will be empowered to go for it!

I'm praying that every group member who is not currently leading a group will be empowered to dive in and be part of a wave of transformation in your group.

I'm praying that God will use each of you to rescue Bible study from "Bible studies" and see the flourishing of your fellow pilgrims on the journey in living out the ***Christ-life***.

Appendix 1 - Powerful Questions

I previously mentioned J. Val Hastings, founder of Coaching4Clergy. In two of his books, *The Next Great Awakening*[27] and *Change Your Questions, Change Your Church*[28], he shares hundreds of questions for a variety of contexts.

I list here some of those (some with slight adaptation) that I think are particularly applicable for getting small groups talking and discussing.

- *What needs more of your attention, right now, today?*
- *What character in this passage do you most resemble or relate to?*
- *Which character would you like to resemble, and why?*
- *What is most important for you to tackle today?*
- *What steps can you take so that your words and actions match?*
- *What can you do to be more effective this week?*
- *What is the one question you need to be asking yourself about this lesson?*
- *What new ways of being are needed for you to move forward?*

---

[27] J. Val Hastings, *The Next Great Awakening: How to Empower God's People with a Coach Approach to Ministry*, 2010, Coaching4Clergy.

[28] J. Val Hastings, *Change Your Questions, Change Your Church: How to Lead with Powerful Questions*, 2012, Coaching4Clergy.

- *What is the most wonderful thing about God that you learned today?*
- *What keeps you from hearing God speak?*
- *What would cause you to jump with joy this week?*
- *What pearls of wisdom could you hand out to others this week?*
- *What's on the back burner that needs to be placed on the front burner?*
- *Why is it so much easier to plan than it is to take action?*
- *What is it costing you to stay the same?*
- *What if your assumptions are wrong?*
- *What are you waiting for?*
- *What has changed the most about you in the past year?*
- *What really empowers you?*
- *How have you experienced the overflow of God's love in the past week?*
- *Ecclesiastes 3:1-8 says there is a time for everything. What time is it for you right now?*
- *What is the greatest lesson you have learned?*
- *What do you need to say goodbye to in order to move forward?*
- *What keeps you up at night?*
- *What will you say "No" to today that will help you say "Yes" to what matters most?*
- *What internal rules and unspoken standards are having a negative impact on you?*
- *What would your life be like if you mustered the courage to do what you already know you need to do?*
- *Who can you forgive today?*

- *When are you most aware of God's amazing love for you?*
- *Who or what is the source of most of your stress?*
- *What would make the biggest difference in your life today?*
- *What is God's deepest desire for you? Your Church?*
- *What would you do differently if your biggest problem were solved?*
- *What will you do to protect your priorities?*
- *What are you most afraid of, and how might that fear be getting in the way?*
- ***What are the things that only you can do this week?***
- ***What are the things that you and others can do this week?***
- ***What are the things that you can do, but choose not to do this week?***
- ***What are the things that you cannot do and never want to do?***
- *Based on the previous four questions, what new information have you gained?*
- *Based on the previous four questions, what will you stop doing and delegate to someone else?*
- *Based on the previous four questions, how will your schedule this week be different?*
- *In what ways are you having the greatest impact on others?*
- *What is the true potential of your church?*
- *What makes you proud to be a part of your church?*
- *What needs to happen for your church to be at its full potential?*

- *What is your contribution to your church being at its full potential?*
- *When is it hardest for you to trust God, as we are invited to do in Proverbs 3:5-6?*[29]
- *What is the decision that you are avoiding?*
- *What would it take to turn up the volume on the still small voice of God?*
- *What consumes your time, to the point that it distracts you from attaining your goals?*
- *What are the action steps that only you can take today?*
- *What beliefs strengthen you?*
- *What makes your church unique?*

---

[29] *Trust in the LORD with all your heart and do not lean on your own understanding. In all your ways acknowledge Him, and He will make your paths straight.* (Proverbs 3:5-6)

Appendix 2 - Tips for Getting a Good Night's Sleep

A simple Google search for "strategies for a good night's sleep" yielded 480,000 results. You can do the same search and get some great information.

My purpose here is to share some things that have been helpful for me in preparing to be at my best to preach, teach, and lead on Sunday mornings. Some are things I've been doing for years. Others are new strategies that I have learned more recently. I am only sharing things here that I have personally tried and know to be effective.

Routines

1. **No caffeine after 4:00 p.m.** Maybe that doesn't affect you. Maybe it does and you just don't know it. Try cutting out caffeine at 4:00 p.m. for 30 days and see if there is any difference in your sleep quality.
2. **Don't stay OUT late on Saturday night.** I mentioned in Chapter 4 that my habit for years has been to decline most invitations on Saturday evenings because of the high priority I place on Sunday morning effectiveness. It is a choice and matter of priorities.
3. **Don't stay UP late on Saturday night.** The fact that you are home early doesn't guarantee a good night's sleep if you stay up late watching TV, surfing the Internet, or even reading. I personally need at least 7 hours of sleep to function at my best. If I know what time I need to get up on Sunday morning to be unhurried, then simple math tells me what time I need to go to bed.

4. **Go to bed at a similar time EVERY night**. Our bodies develop a rhythm for waking, sleeping, eating, and various other activities. The less we interrupt that rhythm, the more we are able to consistently operate at prime effectiveness. I used to believe that I was a "night owl" and I stayed up late almost every night to prove it. On those mornings when it was necessary to get up early, it was really hard. Adjusting my routine to an earlier bedtime has been really helpful for personal productivity AND for my personal spiritual life and the habits that are important to me.

5. **Unplug and disconnect from media at least 30 minutes before bedtime.** There is research that shows how the light from screens (TV, tablet, phone) hinders sleep. Even apart from research, I know how my sleep has been delayed — sometimes for hours — by watching TV (especially channel surfing), checking email, or scrolling through Facebook. It is much easier for me to wind down by reading, and it is better to do it with an actual book than on an e-Reader with a backlight.

6. **A cool, dark room is a much better sleeping atmosphere.** Your own body temperature will give you the definition of cool, but it is easier — and more conducive to sleep — to pull up a blanket because it is cool, than it is to strip something else off because it is too hot. We keep our bedroom at about 68 degrees at night. I have slept with a small pillow or hand towel over my face for years to block light. I recently started wearing a sleep mask and it has been fantastic!

7. **White noise covers a multitude of sleep interrupters.** Early in our marriage I was up half the night trying to find a cricket that would only chirp when all the lights were out and I was back in bed. A box fan that runs 365 nights a year has made it possible to sleep through insects, barking dogs, creaks and groans of an old house, etc. I even have a fan app on

my iPhone so that I can keep the noise going while traveling.

8. **Essential oils as sleep aids.** My wife and I started using essential oils for overall wellness a little over two years ago. I will not make any claims about their effectiveness for anyone else, but we both use a blend each night of Vetiver, Cedar Wood, and Serenity blend[30] and we have both found that our sleep quality has improved.

For times when sleep doesn't come easy or is disturbed

1. **Sometimes a sleep disorder, such as sleep apnea exists.** That is the case for me, so the fact that I use a c-pap machine is both a sleep solution and a routine. If you find yourself awaking often, snoring, and being constantly tired during the day, I encourage you to take a sleep test. Studies have shown some significant health risks associated with sleep apnea.

2. **Deep breathing and meditation.** I have found deep inhaling through about a count of 5, holding for a count of 4, and exhaling through a count of 5, repeated several times can be relaxing. I have also repeated familiar Scripture such as Psalm 23 while maintaining deep steady breathing.

3. **Occupying the busy part of the brain.** When my mind is racing with thoughts of things that are going on in my life, upcoming responsibilities, and situations that keep me from shutting down, I have found success with a couple of strategies.

---

[30] We use doTerra essential oils. Other brands that are certified pure therapeutic grade may be just as effective.

4. **If the problem is going to sleep in the first place**, reading a book that is "light" or devotional in nature can be helpful. Sometimes even novels that keep the mind occupied with story can help me relax. I don't read anything that is "work" or "ministry" related at bedtime because that may actually stimulate more thinking.

5. **If the problem is waking up and not being able to go back to sleep**, I may try the Scripture meditation method. I also count backward from 100 with each deep breath. In and out is one number. If I get all the way from 100 to 0 twice, I figure it is a lost cause and I get up and do something productive and make the best of it. However, it is not unusual for me to begin losing count and drifting off while still in the 90's.

These are strategies and habits that I have found helpful. I don't pretend to be able to diagnose anyone else's sleep issues or to suggest that what works for me will necessarily work for someone else. If these tips are helpful to anyone, I'm happy. If they're not, try the Google search or see your physician. The main thing is to try to make sure that you are getting the rest you need to function at your best physically, emotionally, mentally, and spiritually.

About the Author

Dr. Gerry Lewis (Dr. G) has served, since 2008, as Executive Director of Harvest Baptist Association, a regional network of churches in North Central Texas. For the previous 20 years, he served as senior pastor of two churches.

Author of 5 books (so far), blogger, newspaper columnist, podcaster, church health consultant, leadership coach, entertainer, speaker, and foodie – Dr. G has a full life encouraging and empowering others on their next step toward amazing.

His *Life Matters* blog can be found at drgerrylewis.com

His *Your Church Matters* podcast can be found at drgerrylewis.com/yourchurchmatters

Dr. G lives in Azle, Texas with his wife, Eva Dee (Mrs. Sweetie). They have two grown and married children and two spectacular and perfect grandchildren.

Connect with Dr. G

On Facebook
facebook.com/drgerrylewisauthor

On Twitter
twitter.com/drgerrylewis

On LinkedIn
linkedin.com/in/drgerrylewis

On Instagram
instagram.com/drgerry96

By Email
contactgerrylewis@gmail.com

Other books by Dr. G

30 Days of Wisdom

10 Mistakes Pastorless Churches Make (And recommendations for avoiding them)

Life Matters, Volume 2: 2005-2012

Culture Wars

Available at
www.amazon.com
(search for Dr. Gerry Lewis)

More from Dr. G – FREE INSPIRATION AND ENCOURAGEMENT

1. Free eBook

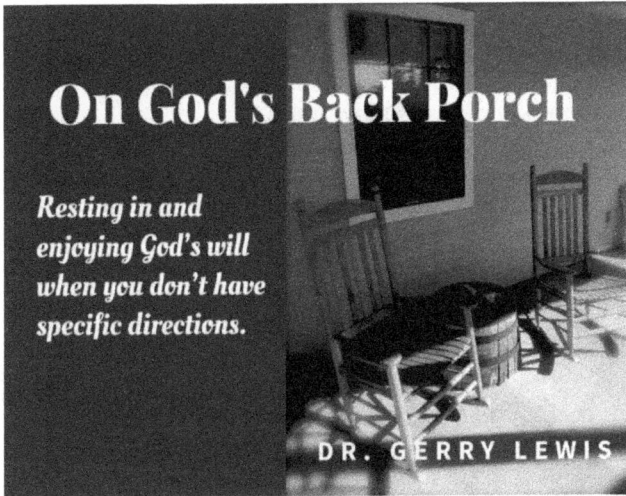

On God's Back Porch

Resting in and enjoying God's will when you don't have specific directions.

DR. GERRY LEWIS

When you think of **God's will**, how do you respond? Do you have a sense of fear or anxiety over what God might require of you? Do you have a sense of fear or anxiety over what might happen if you miss God's **perfect will** or if you make a mistake by **getting ahead of God**? Do words like **sacrifice**, **endurance**, and **duty** come to mind? Do words like **joy**, **contentment**, and **rest** seem foreign or even inappropriate when talking about God's will? Is that really what God's will means?

I'd like to offer a different way of thinking: a different view of God, a different view of His will and our activity. I'll even go so far as to say it is a more Biblically sound view than the graceless, performance-driven burden so many of us have labored under for so long.

This short eBook won't answer every possible question or objection. That's not the purpose. But it will offer another way of thinking. It will offer freedom.

You can't purchase this book anywhere right now, but you can get it for FREE by subscribing to my email newsletter. In addition to getting this eBook, you will also get fresh content delivered directly to your inbox whenever I post something new. You'll get first access to new resources and special "members-only" discounts. You can change your subscription preferences at any time.

To join my subscriber list and get your free eBook, please visit drgerrylewis.com/backporch.

2. A free sample of my most recent book, Culture Wars: *In search of spiritual Jedi*

May the Force Be with You

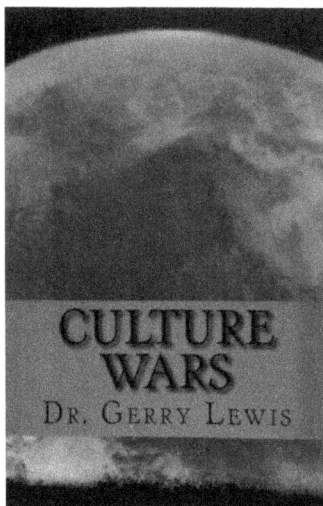

I admit it. I'm a fan of the **Star Wars** movies. Not a "stand in line for hours to see the very first show that opens at midnight, dressed as a Storm Trooper, and knowing the names of all the different Sith lords" fan, I just enjoy the movies. The special effects are amazing and it's kind of silly fun.

But the real reason I like the movies is the Jedi.

The Jedi are an interesting group of people. They are an ascetic group, not concerned with politics, power, prestige, or possessions. They live a life of contemplation and service. Their loyalties are not primarily political, but spiritual. They respect, support, and learn from each other. They know that their success relies on the power of The Force.

And they have these really cool lightsabers! Okay, that's my favorite part. What an amazing weapon! Defensively, they deflect the shots from the Storm Troopers' blasters or the assault of another saber wielded by a devotee of the Dark Side (the big "sithies"). It is a weapon that must be close at hand to be used, but is most effective against a personal attack.

And then there is The Force. It is the true source of power. The Jedi are effective only as they learn to use it. The Sith gain strength as they learn to harness it for the purposes of the Dark Side. Lightsabers are useless to one who does not use the power of the Force.

And *a long time ago in a galaxy far, far away,* the battle for the galaxy rages (and makes a gazillion dollars for George Lucas).

125

CULTURE WARS

The year is 2215 A.D. A twenty-third century moviemaker decides to tell the tale of twenty-first century America. In homage to the most successful movie series of the late twentieth and early twenty-first century, a paragraph of text slowly scrolls from the bottom to the top of the screen against a black, star-lit sky. *A long time ago ...*

How would that paragraph introduce twenty-first century America? What values would be displayed among people? What forces drive the culture? What is the spiritual climate? What unifies people? What divides them?

I'm not sure how future historians will chronicle the world we are living in today. We are writing that history every day as we seek to navigate the sometimes-unfriendly skies of American culture. I do, however, know plenty of people who are convinced that there was a time when the skies were friendlier — people who long for the "good old days" when Judeo-Christian values were the cultural norms. These were times when you would never hear words like *anti-Christian bias, homo-phobic, intolerant, right wing fundamentalist,* or *liberal media.*

At least that's what I'm told. As a child of the 60's and a teenager of the 70's, my own recollections are of a culture in transition. Vietnam and Watergate began the erosion of our trust in political leadership. The ensuing five decades of scandalous behavior among elected officials has done nothing to stop the landslide toward total skepticism. We don't trust anyone anymore.

And what about the church? There was a time when pastors ranked consistently among the most respected people in the community. If you heard it in church, it must be true. If the Christian community is for it, it must be a good thing. And then came outlandish televangelists with more glitz than gospel, the moral and ethical failures of "rock star" preachers, in fighting among evangelicals — and now we trust Christians just about as much as we trust politicians. It seems that the church has lost its voice.

Permit me to ask three vital questions:

1. How much difference is there between churchgoers and non-churchgoers in our culture?

2. Which one is influencing the other more— church or culture?

In other words, when cultural observers take note of the behavior of those who self-identify as Christians, is there any noticeable distinction about them — other than what they do for an hour or two on Sunday mornings? Eugene Peterson writes,

Historically, evangelical Christians have served the church by bringing sharpness and ardor to matters of belief and behavior, insisting on personal involvement, injecting energy and passion, returning daily to the Scriptures for command and guidance, and providing communities of commitment. But presently there is not an equivalent in matters of spirituality. It turns out that we have been affected by our secularizing culture far more than we had realized. Evangelicals have been uncritically internalizing the world's ways and bringing them into churches without anyone noticing. [i]

3. What are we, as the church to do?

If we are indeed *being influenced* by the culture more than we are *influencing* the culture, what's the answer?

Some might suggest *isolation*. This is what Leonard Sweet refers to as the *hunker in the bunker* mentality.[ii] Let's gather up all the people who want to live by traditional Christian values and move away into a commune isolated from the outside world. Then *we'll* be safe and we can just pretend that *they* don't exist. And in so doing, we abandon the culture by removing the remaining Christian influence that exists. No, isolation is not the answer.

Others might suggest *separation*. Let them do their thing and we'll do ours. We'll try to stay as far apart as possible. If our paths have to intersect, we'll nod as politely as possible and continue to remind ourselves (and them) that *we* are not *them*. Certainly, there are aspects of our culture from which we must separate ourselves, but separation is only a partial answer.

The only real answer is *transformation*. Look at the following words of Jesus and especially notice the phrases that I have emphasized.

*I am no longer in the world; and yet **they themselves are in the world**, and I come to You. Holy Father, keep them in Your name, the name which You have given Me, that they may be one even as We are. While I was with them, I was keeping them in Your name which You have given Me; and I guarded them and not one of them perished but the son of perdition, so that the Scripture would be fulfilled. But now I come to You; and these things I speak in the world so that they may have My joy made full in themselves. I have given them Your word; and the world has hated them, because they are not of the world, even as I am not of the world. **I do not ask You to take them out of the world**, but to keep them from the evil one. They are not of the world, even as I am not of the world. Sanctify them in the* *truth; Your word is truth.* **As You sent Me into the world, I also have sent them into the world.** *For their sakes I sanctify Myself, that they themselves also may be sanctified in truth. I do not ask on behalf of these alone, but for those also who believe in Me through their word; that they may all be one; even as You, Father, are in Me and I in You, that they also may be in Us,* **so that the world may believe that You sent Me.**[iii]

Wow! Do you see the purpose that Christians have in the culture? We are to behave in such a way — in the culture — that those who see us will believe the Jesus we claim to know! And in revealing Him, we'll have a hand in transforming the culture back to what God intends.
But, to what do we return? The Bible says,

Do not move an ancient boundary stone set up by your forefathers.[iv]

Someone might read that and say, *See, I told you we needed to go back to the good old days.* But what boundary stones are the right ones to guide twenty-first century life? How about the early American boundary stones — the values of our great-grandparents? Nope, not far enough.

Well, then let's study the early church and the foundations of Christianity and see how they responded to their culture. Still too recent.

Then, obviously, I'm referring to the Ten Commandments. If we would just adopt God's laws as the law of the land, everything would be fine. Not quite there yet.

What, then can possibly bring about the kind of transformation that I'm talking about? Only going all the way back to the heart of God. You see, transformation does not begin with methods, but with relationship.

Then God said, "Let Us make man in Our image, according to Our likeness; and let them rule over the fish of the sea and over the birds of the sky and over the cattle and over all the earth, and over every creeping thing that creeps on the earth." God created man in His own image, in the image of God He created him; male and female He created them.ᵛ

Then the LORD God formed man of dust from the ground, and breathed into his nostrils the breath of life; and man became a living being. The LORD God planted a garden toward the east, in Eden; and there He placed the man whom He had formed. Out of the ground the LORD God caused to grow every tree that is pleasing to the sight and good for food; the tree of life also in the midst of the garden, and the tree of the knowledge of good and evil.ᵛⁱ

Then the LORD God said, "It is not good for the man to be alone; I will make him a helper suitable for him."ᵛⁱⁱ

God created human beings for relationship — relationship with Him and relationship with other humans. Another way of saying that is that God created us for culture. He created us to function within a society that derives its norms — not simply through legislation and powerful enforcement — by means of relationship.

One of the reasons that legislated morality fails is that it does not begin with the heart. A heart that is not right with God and with others may keep the law of the land, and even the letter of the law of God, but it cannot be a part of a culture of Godliness.

For that reason, the assertion of this book is that transformation begins not with culture, but with the church. We will have limited influence on the culture as long as we start with pious proclamations about what *they* are doing wrong. We must start with understanding how *our* hearts reveal a shocking similarity to *theirs*.

For that reason, the **Culture Wars** of which I speak are not the big-ticket morality/world view hot buttons that pit evangelical Christians against liberal hedonists. I am going to reference 8 Cultural Indicators that reveal how much *our* hearts have in common with *theirs*. And once we identify those cultural indicators, what do we do with them? Let us now see the *Return of the Jedi* (and you thought I forgot about them).

Spiritual Jedi

To quote a brilliant author (okay, I'm really reminding you of what I said on the first page of this introduction), the Jedi

> *... are an ascetic group, not concerned with politics, power, prestige, or possessions. They live a life of contemplation and service. Their loyalties are not primarily political, but spiritual. They respect, support, and learn from each other. They know that their success relies on the power of The Force.*

What we need to help transform this culture are some Christ-followers who take the Jedi approach to life from a purely Christian perspective — their spiritual loyalties, their service, their interdependence, their humility — all driven by their total surrender to Jesus Christ.

Of course, we must also point out that these spiritual Jedi know that The Force to which they surrender is the empowering presence of the Spirit of the Living God.

> *These things I have spoken to you while abiding with you. But the Helper, the Holy Spirit, whom the Father will send in My name, He will teach you all things, and bring to your remembrance all that I said to you. Peace I leave with you; My peace I give to you; not as the world gives do I give to you. Do not let your heart be troubled, nor let it be fearful.*[viii]

And did I mention their really cool lightsabers?

Put on salvation as your helmet, and take the sword of the Spirit, which is the word of God.[ix]

For the word of God is living and active. Sharper than any double-edged sword, it penetrates even to dividing soul and spirit, joints and marrow; it judges the thoughts and attitudes of the heart.[x]

This book is issued as a challenge: a challenge to be unsatisfied with cultural capitulation, a challenge to love God more than we love the culture, a challenge to love the culture too much to hand it over to the enemy. A challenge to become spiritual Jedi — entering the battle for the culture, wielding the lightsaber of truth under the direction of the Force of God's Holy Spirit. Take the Jedi's pledge at the end of each chapter. Memorize the lightsaber focus so that you will be constantly ready for battle. Use the questions to discuss with your fellow Jedi. Pray for the guiding power of the Force.

Read on, young padawan (Jedi apprentice)... and may the Force be with you.

Visit drgerrylewis.com/culturewars to get your copy of *Culture Wars*.

Chapter 1: May the Force Be With You

[i] Eugene H. Peterson, *Living the Message: Daily Help for Living the God-Centered Life*, HarperSanFrancisco, 1996, p.243

[ii] I was actually in the audience at a conference when I heard him use this phrase.

[iii] John 17:11-21, *NASU*

[iv] Proverbs 22:28, *NIV*

[v] Genesis 1:26-28, *NASU*

[vi] Genesis 2:7-9, *NASU*

[vii] Genesis 2:18-19, *NASU*

[viii] John 14:25-28, *NASU*

[ix] Ephesians 6:17-18, NLT

[x] Hebrews 4:12, NIV

www.ingramcontent.com/pod-product-compliance
Lightning Source LLC
Chambersburg PA
CBHW031535040426
42445CB00010B/546

O Thou Immortal Deity whose throne

Is in the depth of human thought.

Shelley

Since we live in a Scientific Age

The Myth of God for our Age

Is the Myth of an Infinite Reason.

But, an Infinite Reason implies

An Infinite Person. Thus, the Father of All.

Since, according to Aristotle, we are rational animals,

Our proper lives are, then, spiritual-intellectual lives.

First fruit, self-consciousness: *I am not the not-I.*

Consciousness, an internal awareness

Of an external environment.

*

Self-consciousness, a self-reflective awareness,

A consciousness, or awareness, of awareness.

Perception, to an attentive consciousness,

Suggests essence; consciousness, through the mind,

Thereby moves into things.

There is no perception of the Self

Apart from a cognition of the Self.

To be is to be somewhere.

For rational beings, the universe

Poses a universal question.

Thus, at the risk of a complete,

Or universal failure,

A universal knowledge is needed.

Since our existence is inseparable

From an environment, the ordination of the self

Implies an ordination of the environment.

The will of the self is to think.

Since we are the authors of our assertions,

Our assertions possess a certain authority.

Even as we think what is thought
Is distinguished from all that is not thought.

For the mind to truly know, the heart must also believe.

True thought is a sword.

That ideas are causes,—the whole artifice

Of human civilization is evidence of this.

The intangible produces the tangible,

Thus, the mind, through the instrumentality of the body,

Makes things. Things don't make a mind.

Since thought, in order to establish what is,

Prescinds from the stream of time,

Thinking is our point of contact with Eternity.

—— ——